TRILLIN ON TEXAS

Bridwell Texas History Series

Trillin
ON TEXAS
BY CALVIN TRILLIN

University of Texas Press
AUSTIN

Requests for permission to reproduce material from this work should be sent to:
 Permissions
 University of Texas Press
 P.O. Box 7819
 Austin, TX 78713-7819
 www.utexas.edu/utpress/about/bpermission.html

∞ The paper used in this book meets the minimum requirements of ANSI/NISO
Z39.48-1992 (R1997) (Permanence of Paper).

LIBRARY OF CONGRESS CATALOGING-IN-PUBLICATION DATA

Trillin, Calvin.
 Trillin on Texas / by Calvin Trillin. — 1st ed.
    p.   cm. — (Bridwell Texas history series)
 ISBN 978-0-292-72650-5 (cl. : alk. paper)
 1. Trillin, Calvin—Knowledge—Texas.   2. Texas—Social life and customs—
Humor.   3. Texas—History—Humor.   I. Title.
 PS3570.R5T79   2011
 818'.54—dc22

                                                              2010047578

CONTENTS

INTRODUCTION

Yes, I do have a Texas connection, but, as we'd say in the Midwest, where I grew up, not so's you'd know it. I come from an immigrant family. Although my father sounded like Harry Truman and freely used phrases like "Haven't had so much fun since the hogs ate little sister," he was brought to western Missouri as an infant from a spot in the Tsarist empire which my family always referred to as "near Kiev"—a term that led me to believe as a child that they had lived in the suburbs. As a schoolboy in Kansas City, I read inspiring stories about how new Americans from such places had sailed into New York Harbor, wept at the sight of the Statue of Liberty, and entered the Land of the Free at Ellis Island. I was always puzzled by these stories. In the first decade of the twentieth century, my paternal grandparents—in fact, my father himself—had embarked from Europe and disembarked three weeks later in Galveston, Texas.

By the time I happened upon an explanation for that odd migration pattern, I was an adult. The only one of the immigrant generation still alive was my Uncle Benny Daynofsky—who, in his eighties, was living in a little row house in St. Joseph, Missouri, where he'd gone directly from Galveston in 1907, and devoting much of his time to tending the tomatoes he grew in his backyard. I was lying on the beach, reading a book called *The Provincials*, and I had reached a chapter on the tense relations at the turn of the twentieth century between German Jews in New York—many of whom had established themselves as respectable and prosperous citizens—and the horde of impoverished Eastern European immigrants pouring into the Lower East Side. It said that the financier Jacob Schiff, concerned about the conditions on the Lower East Side "and embarrassed by the image it created for New York's German Jews," pledged half a million dollars in 1906 to the Galveston Movement, which diverted ten thousand immigrants to Galveston.

I sat upright. "Embarrassed!" I said to my wife. "Who is Jacob Schiff to be embarrassed by my Uncle Benny Daynofsky?" My Uncle Benny (actually, my great-uncle) had lived for decades in St. Joe without doing anything at all embarrassing, unless you count making pickled tomatoes too hot for anyone else to eat. Certainly, he'd done nothing as embarrassing as some of the schemes Jacob Schiff cooked up with robber barons like E. H. Harriman. When it comes to rapacious nineteenth-century capitalism, my family's hands are clean. I immediately wrote an essay about discovering, belatedly, how my family got to this country. Its first line was "And who is Jacob Schiff to be embarrassed by my Uncle Benny Daynofsky?"

Any celebration of Uncle Benny's arrival in Texas more than a century ago is, then, clouded a bit by the circumstances, in the way that any celebration of Australia's founding settlers is clouded a bit by the fact that they were convicts. Like those settlers transported to Australia, my forebears were diverted to Texas because they were unwanted somewhere else. As a matter of fact, I later read that before Galveston Movement immigrants left the old country, they had to agree in writing not to remain in Galveston. They were unwanted there, too. It almost goes without saying that they were unwanted "near Kiev." My people did not arrive in the Land of the Free riding waves of acclamation.

As it's turned out, Galveston, where there is a museum devoted to the Galveston Movement, is about the only Texas city that I haven't visited as a reporter. In traveling around the United States doing articles for *The New Yorker*—for fifteen years, I did a piece from somewhere in the country every three weeks—I've often found myself in Texas. This has not been by design. There has simply been a lot going on in Texas—a newspaper war in Dallas, a barbecue discovery in Lexington, a mysterious death in Bastrop County. In writing about other parts of the country, I have often referred to Texas. For instance, in a 1977 piece about the eviction of some poor Filipino residents from a building called the International Hotel in San Francisco—an eviction that had come after an eight and a half month struggle and had at the end required several hundred policemen—I suggested that American cities could be ranked on a left-to-right spectrum according to how long tenants whose eviction had become a cause managed to stay where they were. "Houston is on the far right of the spectrum, with an R.I.B. (Remain in Building) Index of from twenty minutes to an hour," I wrote. "Houston's most powerful citizens are known for a devotion to private property so intense that they see routine planning and zoning as acts of naked confiscation. Houston may also come to mind because at one point in its recent history both the mayor and the police chief conducted real estate businesses on the side."

Wearing my other hat—the jester's cap of someone who attempts to make snide and underhanded jokes about respectable public officials—I have often found myself writing about Texans. Again, this has not been by design. For the past few decades, Texas politicians have found a natural habitat on the national political stage in the way that Dominican shortstops have found a natural habitat in major league baseball. So, you might say that this book is accidental—or, to put it another way, the fault lies with Texas and not with me. I find that a complicated explanation when I'm asked why someone who grew up in Missouri and now lives in New York is publishing a book on Texas. So far, though, I have resisted the temptation to reply, "Well, I happen to come from an old Texas family."

BARBECUE DISCOVERY · CHEERLEADERS · JOHNNY JENKI
IMMIGRATION LAWS · LEXINGTON · CHICANOS · ROSS PER
COWBOY BOOTS · WACO · JOE BOB BRIGGS · MANGLED SYNT
AUSTIN · RACIAL TENSIONS · LBJ SPEECHES · LLOYD BENTS
PERSIAN GULF · CORPUS CHRISTI · DALLAS PUBLIC LIBRA
THE BUSH DYNASTY · BASTROP COUNTY · NEWSPAPER WA
SWEARING LIKE A SAILOR · LARRY McMURTRY · PRESS COR
MOVIE REVIEWS · CRYSTAL CITY · LEGISLATORS · BEAUMON
TEXARKANA · HIGH SCHOOL · BOOK SCOUTS · MOLLY IVI
CRAWFORD RANCH · COURTROOM · BOAT RAMP · PSEUDON
MARIJUANA · RARE BOOKS · THE DIRTY THIRTY · LOBBYIS
BRISKET · $482,662 IN CASH · LA RAZA UNIDA · COLLECTO
THE GREAT SOCIETY · LEE OTIS JOHNSON · HEREFORD STE
HOMECOMING QUEEN · OIL-GLUT RECESSION · PHIL GRAM
GAMBLING · FARM-TO-MARKET 969 · TOOTSIE TOMANE
PROFESSIONAL LIBRARIAN · HUEVOS RANCHEROS · LAWYE
FRANCES (SISSY) FARENTHOLD · NEW BLUE THUNDERBI
DRIVE-IN MOVIES · DRUG SENTENCING · TEXAS OBSERV
PORK BUTT · IMMIGRATION AND NATURALIZATION SERVIC
TEXAS MONTHLY · ALBERTO GONZALES · RODEO CLOW

BARBECUE DISCOVERY · CHEERLEADERS · JOHNNY JENKI
IMMIGRATION LAWS · LEXINGTON · CHICANOS · ROSS PER
COWBOY BOOTS · WACO · JOE BOB BRIGGS · MANGLED SYNTA
AUSTIN · RACIAL TENSIONS · LBJ SPEECHES · LLOYD BENTSE
PERSIAN GULF · CORPUS CHRISTI · DALLAS PUBLIC LIBRA
THE BUSH DYNASTY · BASTROP COUNTY · NEWSPAPER WA
SWEARING LIKE A SAILOR · LARRY McMURTRY · PRESS CORP
MOVIE REVIEWS · CRYSTAL CITY · LEGISLATORS · BEAUMON
TEXARKANA · HIGH SCHOOL · BOOK SCOUTS · MOLLY IVI
CRAWFORD RANCH · COURTROOM · BOAT RAMP · PSEUDONY
MARIJUANA · RARE BOOKS · THE DIRTY THIRTY · LOBBYIS
BRISKET · $482,662 IN CASH · LA RAZA UNIDA · COLLECTO
THE GREAT SOCIETY · LEE OTIS JOHNSON · HEREFORD STEE
HOMECOMING QUEEN · OIL-GLUT RECESSION · PHIL GRAM
GAMBLING · FARM-TO-MARKET 969 · TOOTSIE TOMANET
PROFESSIONAL LIBRARIAN · HUEVOS RANCHEROS · LAWYER
FRANCES (SISSY) FARENTHOLD · NEW BLUE THUNDERBIR
DRIVE-IN MOVIES · DRUG SENTENCING · TEXAS OBSERVE
PORK BUTT · IMMIGRATION AND NATURALIZATION SERVIC
TEXAS MONTHLY · ALBERTO GONZALES · RODEO CLOW
BARBECUE DISCOVERY · CHEERLEADERS · JOHNNY JENKIN

TRILLIN ON TEXAS

BY MEAT ALONE

I approached *Texas Monthly*'s cover story on "The Top 50 BBQ Joints in Texas" this summer the way a regular reader of *People* might approach that magazine's annual "Sexiest Man Alive" feature—with the expectation of seeing some familiar names. There was no reason to think that the list's top tier—the five restaurants judged to be the best in the state—would look much different than it had the last time a survey was published, in 2003. In recent years, Hollywood may have seen some advances in physical training and cosmetic surgery, but barbecue restaurants still tend to retain their lustre much longer than male heartthrobs do. In fact, I've heard it argued that, absent some slippage in management, a barbecue restaurant can only get better over time: many Texas barbecue fanatics have a strong belief in the beneficial properties of accumulated grease.

In discussions of Texas barbecue, the equivalent of Matt Damon and George Clooney and Brad Pitt would be establishments like Kreuz Market and Smitty's Market, in Lockhart; City Market, in Luling; and Louie Mueller Barbecue, in Taylor—places that reflect the barbecue tradition that developed during the nineteenth century out of German and Czech meat markets in the Hill Country of central Texas. (In fact, the title of *Texas Monthly*'s first article on barbecue—it was published in 1973, shortly after the magazine's founding—was "The World's Best Barbecue Is in Taylor, Texas. Or Is It Lockhart?") Those restaurants, all of which had been in the top tier in 2003, were indeed there again in this summer's survey. For the first time, though, a No. 1 had been named, and it was not one of the old familiars. "The best barbecue in Texas," the article said, "is currently being served at Snow's BBQ, in Lexington."

I had never heard of Snow's. That surprised me. Although I grew up in Kansas City, which has a completely different style of barbecue, I have always kept more or less au courant of Texas barbecue, like a sports fan who is almost monomaniacally obsessed with basketball but glances over at the N.H.L. standings now and then just to see how things are going. Reading that the best barbecue in Texas was at Snow's, in Lexington, I felt like a *People* subscriber who had picked up the "Sexiest Man Alive" issue and discovered that the sexiest man alive was Sheldon Ludnick, an insurance adjuster from Terre Haute, Indiana, with Clooney as the runner-up.

An accompanying story on how a Numero Uno had emerged, from three hundred and forty-one spots visited by the staff, revealed that before work began on the 2008 survey nobody at *Texas Monthly* had heard of Snow's, either. Lexington, a trading town of twelve hundred people in Lee County, is only about fifty miles from Austin, where *Texas Monthly* is published, and Texans think nothing of driving that far for lunch—particularly if the lunch consists of brisket that has been subjected to slow heat since the early hours of the morning. *Texas Monthly* has had a strong posse of barbecue enthusiasts since its early days. Griffin Smith, who wrote the 1973 barbecue article and is now the executive editor of the *Arkansas Democrat-Gazette*, in Little Rock, was known for keeping a map of the state on his wall with pushpins marking barbecue joints he had been to, the way General Patton might have kept a map marked with spots where night patrols had probed the German line. I could imagine the staffers not knowing about a superior barbecue restaurant in East Texas; the Southern style of barbecue served there, often on a bun, has never held much interest for Austin connoisseurs. But their being unaware of a top-tier establishment less than an hour's drive away astonished me.

I know some of the *Texas Monthly* crowd. In fact, I once joined Greg Curtis, the former editor, and Steve Harrigan, a novelist who's had a long association with the magazine, on a pilgrimage to Lockhart, which some barbecue fans visit the way the devout of another sort walk the Camino de Santiago. I know Evan Smith, who was the editor of the magazine when this latest barbecue survey was published and has since been promoted to a position that might be described as boss of bosses. I couldn't imagine Smith jiggering the results for nefarious purposes—say, telling his staff to declare a totally unknown barbecue place the best in Texas simply as a way of doing what some magazine editors call "juicing up the story." I took him at his word when, a few months after the list was published, he told me how Snow's had been found. His staff had gone through the letters written after the 2003 survey complaining about the neglect of a superior specialist in pork ribs or the inclusion of a place whose smoked sausage wasn't fit for pets—what Smith, who's from Queens, refers to as "Dear Schmuck letters."

He did acknowledge that his decision to name a No. 1—rather than just a top tier, as in the previous barbecue surveys—came about partly because everyone was so enthusiastic about Snow's product but partly because its story was so compelling. Smith himself was not in a position to confirm the quality of the product. Being from Queens is not the only handicap he has had to surmount in his rise through the ranks of Texas journalism: he has been a vegetarian for nearly twenty-five years. (The fact that he is able to resist the temptation presented by the aroma of Texas pit barbecue, he has said, is a strong indication that he will never "return to the dark side.") As a longtime editor, though, he knew a Cinderella story when he saw one. It wasn't just that Snow's had been unknown to a Texas barbecue fancy that is notably mobile. Snow's proprietor, Kerry Bexley, was a former rodeo clown who worked as a blending-facility operator at a coal mine. Snow's pit master, Tootsie Tomanetz, was a woman in her early seventies who worked as the custodian of the middle school in Giddings, Texas—the Lee County seat, eighteen miles to the south. After five years of operating Snow's, both of them still had their day jobs. Also, Snow's was open only on Saturday mornings, from eight until the meat ran out.

M y conversation with Evan Smith took place in a Chevrolet Suburban travelling from Austin toward Lexington. I'd been picked up at my hotel at 7:20 A.M. The *Texas Monthly* rankings had attracted large crowds to Snow's, and, even four months later, we weren't taking any chances. Greg Curtis and Steve Harrigan were with Smith in the back seats. Harrigan was one of the people who, having been tipped off between the time the feature was completed and the time the magazine came out, hurried over to Snow's like inside traders in possession of material information not available to the general public. He seemed completely unrepentant. "I took my brother and brother-in-law and son-in-law and nephew," he said, smiling slyly. Next to me in the front seat, Paul Burka was doing the driving. Greg Curtis once reminded me that "all barbecue experts are self-proclaimed," but *Texas Monthly* had enough faith in Burka's expertise to send him to Snow's late in the selection process as what Smith calls "the closer." It was up to Burka to confirm or dismiss the judgment of the staffer whose assigned territory for the survey included Lexington, and of Patricia Sharpe, the editor in charge of the project, and of a second staffer sent in as a triple-check. Some people at the magazine had predicted that Burka wouldn't like Snow's barbecue simply because it bore Pat Sharpe's imprimatur. "Paul thinks Pat's judgment of restaurants is fancy and white tablecloth and Pat thinks Paul is a philistine," I heard from the back seat. "And they're both right."

When I spoke to Pat Sharpe a couple of days later, she bristled at the accusation that she is a person of elevated taste. "I'll eat barbecue in the rattiest joint there is," she said in her own defense. Burka, on the other hand, seemed unconcerned about being called a philistine. He is a large man with a white mustache and a midsection that reflects a forty-year interest in Texas barbecue. Having grown up in Galveston, which is not a barbecue center, he innocently started eating what he now describes as "'barbecue' that was one step removed from roast beef" while he was a student at Rice, in Houston; he had his true conversion experience on a trip to Lockhart with Griffin Smith in 1967, when they were both in law school at the University of Texas. Burka, who worked for five years in the Texas state legislature, writes about politics for *Texas Monthly*. Speaking to him as the Suburban rolled toward Lexington, I was reminded of the Austin brought to life in "The Gay Place," Billy Lee Brammer's marvelous 1961 novel about an L.B.J.-like governor called Arthur (Goddam) Fenstermaker. That Austin was essentially a two-company town—the university and the state government—and I always pictured those connected with both companies sharing irreverent observations of the passing scene while consuming a lot of beer in the back of Scholz's beer garden. It is an Austin that is sometimes difficult to discern in a much larger city of slick office buildings and computer-company headquarters and the mother church of Whole Foods, which actually offers barbecue in the meat department of its Austin stores. ("Organic barbecue," Burka muttered, when somebody brought that up.)

The first time Burka went to Lexington to check out Snow's, he arrived just before noon. "It looked like it had never been open," he said. "It was deserted." When he finally got there at a time when meat was still available, he was convinced. In fact, he was rhapsodic, particularly concerning the brisket ("as soft and sweet as cookie dough") and the pork butt. Smith believed that Burka's description of the latter—"the butt was tender and yielding"—was in need of some editing, but, without having to consume any critters personally, he was persuaded by Burka's report. Snow's was to be named the best barbecue in Texas, and Evan Smith never had any doubt about what would happen as soon as that designation was on the newsstands. "I basically said, 'Congratulations and I'm sorry,'" he told me, "because I knew what would happen."

"That brings up the subject of remorse," I said.

"You mean remorse on their part?" Smith asked.

"No, remorse on your part—remorse for having turned the place into an ugly scene."

"We don't publish *Best-Kept Secrets Monthly*," Smith said, as he got out of Burka's Suburban. He sniffed confidently, presumably to reassure himself that, despite the aroma, he would have no trouble limiting himself to coleslaw and potato salad. Then he marched across the street toward Snow's BBQ.

Regular consumers of Hill Country–style Texas barbecue know what to expect when they walk into an establishment that is said to offer the real article. I had never been to Louie

Mueller's, in Taylor, before this trip, but when Greg Curtis and I went there the day before the Snow's outing for what we referred to as some warmup barbecue, the place looked familiar. At a Texas barbecue joint, you normally pick up a tray at the counter and order meat from one person and sides from another. The person doling out the meat removes it from the smoker and carves it himself. It is sold by the pound—often brisket and pork ribs and sausage and beef ribs and chicken and, in some places, clod (beef shoulder). The carver serves it on some variety of butcher paper. If, despite having worked with smoke in his eyes for many years, he is of a generous nature, as the carvers at Mueller's are known to be, he might slice off a piece of a brisket's darkened outside—what would be called in Kansas City a burnt end—and, before you've ordered anything, place it on your tray as a small gesture. (Given the quality of Mueller's brisket, it is a gesture that can make a traveller feel immensely pleased about being back in Texas.) A couple of slices of packaged white bread are also included. Usually, the only way to have a brisket sandwich in central Texas is to make your own.

A Texas barbecue joint is likely to have neon beer signs on the walls, and those walls are likely to have been darkened by years of smoke. At Mueller's, a cavernous place in a former school gym, there is a large bulletin board festooned with business cards, and most of the cards by now look like specks of brownish parchment. In a restaurant serving Hill Country barbecue, there may be bottles of sauce on the tables, but the meat does not come out of the pits slathered in sauce. I remember a sign at Kreuz Market announcing that the management provided neither sauce nor salads nor forks. In central Texas, you don't hear a lot of people talking about the piquancy of a restaurant's sauce or the tastiness of its beans; discussions are what a scholar of the culture might call meat-driven.

Geographically, Lexington is not in the Hill Country—it's in ranch land, northeast of Austin—but ethnically it is. Burka told me that a politician from Lee County once said to him, "It's the Germans against the Czechs, and the Americans are the swing vote." Snow's BBQ turned out to have the sort of layout found in a place like Kreuz Market, except in miniature. It's a small dark-red build-

ing that has room for a counter and six tables—with a few more tables outside, near the cast-iron smokers that in Texas are referred
to as pits, even if they're not in the ground. A sign listed what
meats were available, all for $8.45 a pound: sausage, brisket, pork,
pork ribs, and chicken. The sides offered were "Mrs. Patschke's
homemade coleslaw and potato salad," plus free beans. There
were only a couple of people ahead of us in line. Burka stepped up
to the counter to order.

"Are there five of you?" the young woman slicing the meat
asked, as Burka tried to figure out how many pounds we needed.

"Well," Burka said, glancing at Evan Smith. "Four, really. One is
... he has a big meal coming up."

"You're ashamed of your friend," I whispered to Burka. "You've
abandoned him."

"I just couldn't say the V-word," Burka said. He looked sheep-
ish—not, I would guess, a normal look for him.

I had warned the *Texas Monthly* crowd that if they were looking for confirmation of their ranking by an objective outlander,
someone from Kansas City was not likely to provide it. A jazz fan
taken to a rock concert might admire the musical technique, but
he probably wouldn't make an ecstatic rush to the stage. As we sat
down at one of the outside tables, under a galvanized-tin covering,
I told them that they could expect the sort of response that a proud
young father I know has received during the past year or so whenever he e-mails me pictures of his firstborn: "A perfectly adequate
child." Still, what Burka had ordered was good enough to make
me forget that we were eating a huge meal of barbecue at a time
on Saturday morning when most people were starting to wonder
what they might rustle up for breakfast once they bestirred themselves. I particularly liked the brisket, although I couldn't attest
that it was as soft and sweet as cookie dough. In Kansas City, it is
not customary to eat cookie dough.

Although Snow's hours may seem odd to a city dweller, they
seem normal in Lexington. Saturday is traditionally when
farmers and ranchers from the surrounding area come into town,

and at twelve-thirty every Saturday there is a cattle auction in yards that are just down the street from Snow's. From 1976 to 1996, in fact, Tootsie Tomanetz, who is known far and wide in Lee County as Miss Tootsie, served barbecue every Saturday at a meat market that she and her husband ran in Lexington. Miss Tootsie's husband is half Czech and half German. She was born Norma Frances Otto, German on both sides, and her father liked to say that when she married she went from having a last name that could be spelled backward or forward to having one that couldn't be spelled at all. Before the Tomanetzes opened their store, Miss Tootsie had put in ten years tending the pits at City Meat Market, in Giddings. In other words, Kerry Bexley, who's forty-one, could have a certainty about Miss Tootsie's gift that was based on having eaten her barbecue virtually all his life.

After lunch, if that's what you call a large meal of meat that you finish just before 9 A.M., I had a chat about Snow's origins with its management team. We talked near the pits, so Miss Tootsie could pull off sausage links now and then. "I felt like with her name and barbecue and my personality with people we could make it work," Bexley told me. He's a short, outgoing man whose résumé includes—in addition to rodeo clown—prison guard, auctioneer, real-estate agent, and shopkeeper. He already had the location— a place where he'd run a farm and ranch store in 1992. The name came from a nickname he'd had since before he was born. According- ing to the family story, his brother, then four years old, was asked whether he was hoping for the new baby to be a boy or a girl, and he replied, not unreasonably, that he would prefer a snowman. Kerry (Snowman) Bexley and Miss Tootsie opened Snow's in March of 2003—Bexley had built the pits—and it did well from the start. "For the most part, we cooked two to three hundred pounds of meat," Bexley told me. "We sold out by noon."

In the weeks after the *Texas Monthly* feature was published, Snow's went from serving three hundred pounds of meat every Saturday to serving more than a thousand pounds. At eight in the morning—six or seven hours after Miss Tootsie had arrived to be- gin tending the pits—there was already a line of customers, some of whom had left home before dawn. Bexley said that one Saturday morning, when there were ninety people waiting outside, a local resident asked permission to gather signatures along the line for a petition, only to return a few minutes later with the information that there wasn't one person there from Lee County. Some locals expressed irritation at being shut out of their own barbecue joint. At times, Bexley and Miss Tootsie felt overwhelmed. There were moments, they say, when they wished that the tasters from *Texas Monthly* had never shown up. Then Bexley added three brisket pits, Miss Tootsie got some help, Snow's for a time quit taking pre-orders by phone except for locals, and the amount of meat prepared every Saturday levelled off to about eight hundred pounds.

Most of the time, Bexley and Miss Tootsie are grateful for the additional business. Not long after the survey appeared, Snow's BBQ started selling T-shirts that had on them not only "Voted #1 BBQ in Texas" but a motto that Bexley's wife had suggested—"Smokin' the good stuff." Looking around for a way to extend the newly famous Snow's brand without sacrificing the quality of the product, Bexley has hit on mail order, and is hoping to have that under way soon. Snow's already has a Web site. Bexley and Miss Tootsie are also pleased by the personal recognition. They've worked hard. Most people in Lee County work hard without anybody's noticing. Whether or not Kerry Bexley and Tootsie Tomanetz ever feel able to give up their day jobs, they have received the sort of pure validation that doesn't come to many people, no matter what their field of endeavor.

"Miss Tootsie gets some recognition now for what she's actually done all her life," Bexley said. "She's now"—he turned to Miss Tootsie—"seventy-four? Excuse me for asking."

"No, I'm just seventy-three," Miss Tootsie said, smiling. "You add a year every time."

"What did you do when you heard that you were No. 1?" I asked.

"When we found out we were No. 1," Bexley said, "we just set there in each other's arms and we bawled."

—2008

THE DYNASTICKS

When I read that the Bush family doesn't like to be called a dynasty, I figured that the word must remind them of *Dynasty*, the '80s soap that was known for the sort of clothing the Bushes would consider unseemly and the sort of intensely personal discussions the Bushes, who pride themselves on being nonintrospective, would find embarrassing. From the impression we've been given about Bush family get-togethers at Kennebunkport, Me., the introduction of a *Dynasty* sort of problem at the dinner table—let's say the sabotage of a family oil rig, in which the suspect is a nephew who might be gay, unless he's the one who raped his sister-in-law, the blackmailer—would result in the patriarch's confirming that family friends had already been called for an infusion of capital and then getting back to the conversation about Dallas' chances to make it to the next Super Bowl.

It turns out that what the Bushes dislike about being called a dynasty is the implication of power being passed along rather than individuals earning it on their own. Few people can be as blithe about such matters as a jovial friend of mine who presided over a large family business and claimed that when he introduced his son to those who would supervise him in the traditional break-in job, he said, "I want you to treat him the same way you'd treat any employee who will some day own this company."

Still, the Bushes fit the accepted definition of a dynasty. They do pass down power. (In fact, reformers must be pondering what there is about our political system that caused both major parties in 2000 to nominate candidates who patently wouldn't have been there if their fathers had been in another line of work.) Also, the Bushes hold political beliefs as a family: what they believe may have changed since the Wall Street Republicanism of Senator Prescott Bush, but everybody seems to have changed in step. And, like all other dynasties, they could have been choked off a number of times—most notably in 1980, when George the Elder had been whomped by Ronald Reagan and was faced with returning to Texas, having just about run out of offices to which he could be appointed.

I sometimes try to imagine lunch at Kennebunkport on the day in 1980 when George H. W. Bush declared himself an opponent of abortion in order to become Ronald Reagan's running mate.

"Guys," the head of the family says to his grown sons, "I've decided that, despite all the money the family has poured into Planned Parenthood all these years, abortion is not a matter of a woman's right to control her own body, after all. It's baby killing, pure and simple."

"Fine, Pop," Jeb says. "Sounds good. Baby killing it is."

"O.K., Pop," George W. says. "Whatever. Can I use the boat this afternoon?"

At this moment, it is clear that the Bush family has seized the opportunity to survive as a dynasty. George H. W. Bush turns to look seriously at his wife.

"Bar," he says, "I believe this is the best apple cobbler I've ever put in my mouth."

—2001

MYSTERY MONEY

It came to light because of a bad left turn. This was in Waco, Texas, on a cold night at the end of January in 1977. At about ten-thirty, a new blue Thunderbird—so new that it still had a temporary paper license plate taped on the back window—stopped at a red light on Valley Mills Drive, a wide double lane dominated by strip shopping centers and car dealerships and franchise restaurants. The overhead traffic light turned green, and the Thunderbird turned left onto Bosque Boulevard, the driver apparently not having noticed that a separate light across the intersection governed left turns. That light was red. A police cruiser happened to be coming down Valley Mills Drive from the opposite direction, and its driver, a young Waco policeman named Edwin Byford, saw the bad left turn. Byford signalled the Thunderbird to the curb. There were two teen-age boys inside. The driver, who gave his name as Dean Moore, did not have a driver's license. He was vague about where he lived. Byford radioed for a backup, on the assumption that he was going to take the boys into custody. Within a few minutes, there were four policemen at the scene, and both of the boys were in handcuffs. The police thought that the Thunderbird might have been stolen. According to the temporary license, it had been bought that very day in Dallas, ninety miles to the north. The name listed on the license as the buyer did not match the name on either boy's identification. An identification card shown by the boy in the passenger's seat said that his name was Percy Garcia and that he lived in Alice—a South Texas county seat that is four hundred miles from Dallas. The boys were taken to Police Headquarters. The Thunderbird was searched. There remains some dispute about whether it was searched right there on Bosque Boulevard or back at Waco Police Headquarters. There is no dispute about what was discovered in two suitcases in the trunk. The suitcases held four hundred and eighty-two thousand six hundred and sixty-two dollars in cash.

The boys said they had found it. For a time, they didn't really offer any further explanation of how they happened to come into possession of almost half a million dollars. Then, for a time, the boy who had been driving—a fifteen-year-old whose real name turned out to be James Dean Bridges—offered too many explanations. Dean (as he was called) started by saying that he and Percy were Mafia runners from Chicago heading for a marijuana pickup in Mexico. The Waco policemen who were questioning Dean and Percy were not well-travelled men, but they thought it was safe to assume that people hired as runners by the Chicago Mafia are not ordinarily teen-agers with strong Texas accents. The police were also unimpressed by Dean's story that he and Percy had found the money in an old man's back yard in Chicago. Even Dean didn't sound as if he believed the one about having robbed a train in Georgia. Finally, Dean said that his father was involved in drug-dealing and had buried the money on his ranch, outside Alice. The police found that one rather believable.

Dean's story about his father, being only one more unproved story, was not made public. The early news accounts described the cash in a phrase that stuck with it in the years that followed— Mystery Money. There was some speculation in the press about where the money might have come from, but from the start what appealed to the press and to the public was the wondrous tale of two breezy Texas boys who happened to run across half a million dollars in cash. The essential elements of that tale were not in dispute: the boys had unearthed a red ice chest full of money on Dean's father's ranch, they had made their way to Dallas by bus, they had handed out several thousand dollars to people who had rendered them a service or told them a particularly compelling hard-luck story, they had managed to buy a new Thunderbird, and they were on their way to even more fantastic adventures when reality intruded in the person of Officer Edwin Byford. The early headlines used phrases like "MYSTERY MONEY BOYS" and "RICH KIDS" and "ROBIN HOODLIKE EXPLOITS" and "CASH CAPER."

"We started billing it as an adventure from the beginning," Charles Barrera, an amiable young lawyer from Alice, who represented Percy Garcia, said recently. "From the beginning, people were saying it was a Huck Finn–Tom Sawyer type of adventure." Most lawyers in South Texas county seats do not talk about billing except in the sense that bookkeepers might talk about it, but then most lawyers in South Texas county seats have never negotiated movie deals. Within a few days of the bad left turn in Waco, Chuck Barrera and George Shaffer, a Corpus Christi lawyer, who represented Dean, found themselves talking about options and points and control of the T-shirt rights. In Barrera's mind, how the adventure would play as a movie was intertwined with how it would play in court. He and Shaffer were contending that if nobody came forward to claim the money it belonged to Dean Bridges and Percy Garcia—a contention that was bound to be tested before a jury. What the boys had going for them, Barrera figured, was their appeal as teen-agers on a lark—zany, perhaps a bit irresponsible, but basically as charming as Huck and Tom. Within a few weeks of the arrest in Waco, Barrera was working closely in Alice with the buyer of the movie option, a man from California named Antonio Santillan, in the hope that the movie would be out before the boys had to argue their case in court. "I wanted the full impact felt by the American public," he says. "I wanted a swelling of sympathy for these boys." Barrera believed that there was a natural sympathy not simply for the boys but also for the case they were arguing. Their claim to the money was based partly on an appealing folk notion that also happens to be a rule of common law—finders keepers.

One argument against the finders-keepers claim was apparent from that first round of questioning at the Waco police station: Can someone be said to have found something if he already knew it was there? In the questioning in Waco and in later testimony, Dean offered several stories to explain what had inspired him to begin digging precisely where he dug—in a quail pen not far from the ranch house. He said that he had once seen a shadowy figure burying something there. He said that he had once helped his father dig up money from the quail pen during a flood, helped dry it out by spreading it all over the kitchen, and then helped rebury it in the ice chest. He said that some chickens he kept in the quail pen had exposed the top of the ice chest while scratching in the earth one day. Dean's lawyer, George Shaffer, saw such discrepancies as perfectly understandable once the Huck Finn model was accepted. His exchange with a Waco police officer named D. L. Chambers during the taking of Chambers' deposition reflected the difference between what the boys' attorneys saw as the sort of adventure Mark Twain might have written and what the authorities insisted on treating as grim, unappealing reality.

"When young men such as this are on a frolic, they don't usually tell the exact straight of a tale that they're telling, do they?" asked Shaffer, who tends to talk in a down-home, storytelling way.

"I always did," Officer Chambers replied.

E ventually, everyone was satisfied that the boys were telling more or less the straight of the tale about the day they unearthed the money. It had started with a long-distance call from Dean to Percy, a good friend from Alice High School. Dean and his father had gone to the quarter-horse races in another part of the state, there had been an argument over Dean's smoking, and his father had slapped him. Dean wanted to come home. He needed someone to pick him up at the bus station in Corpus Christi, forty-five miles east of Alice. Percy recruited John Rose, a classmate who had access to a pickup truck. From the bus station, the boys drove to the ranch, and the three of them dug up the ice chest. After Dean got some clothes and a 9-mm. pistol from inside the house and Percy stopped for a couple of suitcases, they were ready to take off. John Rose had decided not to go along, but he agreed to drive Dean and Percy to the bus station. Dean gave him four thousand dollars for his trouble. "He seemed satisfied," Dean said later. "I wasn't stingy with it."

Percy and Dean took the overnight Trailways to Dallas. They checked into the Baker Hotel—a large old downtown hotel that had declined somewhat since the days when it could be compared with the Adolphus, a Dallas institution just across the street. After a short rest, they headed for Sears. Bluejeans were on sale, and they bought six pairs. They also bought a Polaroid camera and a cassette recorder. Then they started to wrestle with the problem of how two teenagers without a driver's license between them were going to buy a car.

That problem was solved during a stop at the Wild West Saloon, a bar on the edge of downtown Dallas. Although its name and its elaborate neon sign may have made the Wild West sound like one of those theme bars designed for tourists and college kids, it was in fact a dark and unadorned place with a cement floor and a crowd of afternoon drinkers nobody could mistake for fraternity boys. A few of them told Dean and Percy hard-luck stories. "They said they're just broke," Dean recalled later. "They're drinking all their money. Their wives are mad at them. All that stuff." Dean and Percy handed out a thousand or so. One of the people in the bar was a young black man named Gilbert Bailey. He spoke in an accent that the boys had never heard from any black man in South Texas; they remember him as Brazilian, but he might have been from some place like Jamaica or Barbados. Bailey was asked if he would be willing to buy Dean and Percy a car. Apparently, he thought at first that they were joking. Then Percy displayed a wad of cash he had in his boot. Then Dean displayed the 9-mm. pistol. Then the three of them went off to Gus Shaffar Ford.

Dean and Percy decided on a metallic-blue Thunderbird that was on the showroom floor. It did not quite match their standards of flash, but it seemed to be about the best that Gus Shaffar Ford had to offer. Bailey was given the money, and the boys waited just outside the showroom. Bailey came out now and then for consultations or for more cash—including a couple of thousand for him to keep. It took less than half an hour for Bailey to close the deal and drive the Thunderbird out of the showroom. Just outside, Percy and Dean hopped in. In the years since, some people have expressed amazement that a young man with a foreign accent, in constant consultation with two teen-agers who were loitering just outside, could peel off hundred-dollar bills for a new Thunderbird and drive it away without any questions being asked. Dean, for one, saw nothing remarkable about it. "If you got money, they don't ask nothing," he said recently. "They just give you the receipt."

During another stop at Sears, the boys ditched Bailey and headed for I-35. "We were just going up North," Dean said not long ago. "I had never been up there." The specific destination that Dean had in mind was Chicago. "That's as far north as you could go," he explained later. "There were a lot of places I planned on stopping at in between." The I-35 interchange was confusing—what Dean has described as "a spaghetti bowl." Dean headed the Thunderbird in the wrong direction—not north toward Chicago and its Mafia runners but south toward Waco, a city known in Texas for Baylor University and for a strict interpretation of how Southern Baptists are supposed to behave in order to stay right with their God. Dean says that they got faulty directions. One lawyer who has worked on the Mystery Money case and treasures it partly for its entertainment value likes to think that the Thunderbird's route was set by a higher authority. "Can't you just see it?" he said recently. "Retribution! I like to think that God just took that car and turned it right around. Right around toward—of all places—Waco."

In Alice, about the only thing anyone found mysterious about the Mystery Money was whose drug haul it was. Alice, the seat of Jim Wells County, is a city of twenty thousand people on the sparsely populated plains of South Texas. Except for a couple of large, modern bank headquarters, its commercial district consists of a quiet downtown of one-story buildings and a long, franchise-clogged double lane heading east toward Corpus. From the air, it must look like a sleepy beast with a neon tail. Alice was named after the daughter of a founder of the King Ranch, which is nearby, but since the thirties its economy has centered on oil and gas rather than cattle. Its chief annual event is not a rodeo but the Southwest Energy Exposition. Alice has sometimes been known as the Hub City of South Texas. It lies squarely on Highway 281, where traffic comes straight north from the Mexican border, an hour and a half away, and either continues toward San Antonio or branches off to Corpus Christi. By the time Dean and Percy were stopped for the bad left turn in Waco, some people in Texas had started referring to Highway 281 as Marijuana Alley.

Alice never acquired the sort of reputation that clings to some of
the Rio Grande Valley border towns, where manifestations of un-
explained wealth became practically a tourist attraction several
years ago. Still, a resident who has kept his eyes open can point
out an impressive house or two that is, as they say in South Texas,
"made out of drugs." Even a resident who hadn't been paying
much attention wouldn't have had much doubt about what sort
of business produced an ice chest full of cash buried on a rather
remote ranch a few miles from Highway 281.

Alice is not the easiest place to sell the romance of a teen-age
frolic. In South Texas, a lot of people seem to assume a base and
probably corrupt motive for almost any human act, and history
has tended to bear them out. Jim Wells County, in fact, has a secure place in the sort of political lore that makes South Texas long
on cynics. In the primary election of 1948—or, to put it more precisely, somewhat after everyone else assumed that the election
of 1948 was over—Jim Wells County produced the famous Box
13, which contained just enough votes to elect Lyndon Johnson a
United States senator, and to earn him the name Landslide Lyndon. Only ten miles west of Alice is San Diego, the seat of Duval
County—once the headquarters of a political boss known as the
Duke of Duval, whose exploits included a bitter struggle to add
Jim Wells County to his duchy. The Duke's machine is no longer
intact—the Duke, George Parr, shot himself in 1975—but people
in Alice still sometimes refer to San Diego as being "behind the
mesquite curtain." The whole area has a reputation for producing
politicians whose rascality and ferocity could drive a Chicago al-
derman into the arms of the reformers. South Texas is the sort of
place where a lawman who didn't arrest a lot of drug dealers might
be assumed to be on the take and where a lawman who was particularly zealous about drug arrests might be assumed to be dem-
onstrating how worthwhile it would be to put him there. When a
woman who has lived in Alice for some years was asked recently
why the sheriff who was in office at the time of the Mystery Money
made so many arrests of people carting drugs through Jim Wells
County on Highway 281, she said, without hesitation, "He wanted

their cars." It is true that the sheriff and a former district attorney and several others were indicted for giving the confiscated cars to friends and political supporters. The charges were dropped when the sheriff announced his resignation for reasons of health, though, and it was widely noted in Jim Wells County that the former district attorney involved had once helped indict the county judge. One citizen summed up the entire incident for a visiting reporter from the Dallas *Times Herald* as "just politics."

The Garcias were well known in Alice. Percy's father had retired as a postman and got work as a security guard. One of Percy's uncles was a justice of the peace. Although the Waco police described Percy as "Hispanic male," the description must have been inspired more by his name than by his appearance. He has green eyes and brown hair—his mother is only half Mexican-American—and he understands Spanish a lot better than he speaks it. In 1977, Percy Garcia was a fairly cheerful sixteen-year-old—a husky boy whose main interest in school was the prospect of making the baseball team—but nobody in Alice ever mistook him for Huck Finn. As Barrera sometimes puts it, "the boys were not model students." In school, Percy had disciplinary problems. When the Waco police noticed a bulge in Percy's clothing during questioning, they discovered that he had stuffed into his pants a plastic bag that contained not only seven thousand dollars but an ounce and a half of marijuana.

"Why did you have the marijuana?" George Shaffer later asked Percy in court.

"Just a habit, I guess," Percy said.

Dean was not as well known around town. He had been raised in Corpus Christi, by his mother and stepfather. He carried his stepfather's surname, through adoption. When he was thirteen, though, he had decided that he wanted to live with his natural father, James Hiroms, who was a sheet-metal worker by trade. A year or so later, he and his father moved to the ranch near Alice. Hiroms kept some cattle and had a feed store in Corpus and owned some quarter horses. In South Texas, a sheet-metal worker with enough capital to buy a store or a ranch or some quarter horses may raise some suspicion about the true source of his income. Those who were suspicious of James Hiroms felt their suspicions confirmed when he made no claim for the money found on his ranch and went to jail briefly rather than answer a grand jury's questions about it.

The City of Waco found that having nearly five hundred thousand dollars in cash was a burden. The money had to be kept somewhere. It had to be guarded. It represented a potential liability if it got lost or if the city was sued for giving it to the wrong parties. A lot of parties were asking for it. Dean and Percy, of course, said that it belonged to them. The State of Texas said that it would claim the cash under the laws of escheat, by which property or money that has no legal owner reverts to the state after seven years. McLennan County, of which Waco is the seat, put in a claim under a Texas provision that awards counties any unclaimed property seized by a state or county police officer—a provision that lawyers familiar with the case tended to think of as considerably less compelling than the one relied on by the state. Early in the interrogation of Dean and Percy at the Waco police station, the police questioners had been joined by two men from the Internal Revenue Service, and within a few days the I.R.S. had notified both Waco and the boys that the federal government considered itself entitled to a large chunk of the cash.

The City of Waco did not claim the money—a decision that still puzzles some of the lawyers connected with the case. "We could not figure out anything that would give us a right to it," the city attorney said recently. In an effort to free itself from the problems and expense involved in holding the stakes, the city interpleaded the Mystery Money into state court—a legal procedure by which a party can simply hand money over to a court and ask the judge to assume the responsibility of deciding who should have it. The presence of the I.R.S. caused the case to be removed to federal court, and lawyers began the depositions and motions and discoveries leading up to a trial. A lot of people who had read about the Mystery Money didn't think a trial was necessary. Felipe Reyna, who, as McLennan County district attorney, made the decision to claim the money for the county, has said that his decision was unpopular not only because some people considered the county's legal argument farfetched but also because "everybody thought the money should go to these two children."

That was precisely the sort of thinking that Chuck Barrera hoped to encourage—with the help of Antonio Santillan, who had flown from California to South Texas as soon as the movie deal was made. In Alice, Santillan struck everyone as a perfect Hollywood type—curly hair, designer jeans, and big plans. He spent hours at the Sheraton Marina, in Corpus Christi, with Dean and Percy, taping their recollections. He scouted locations in Alice. He held a news conference at the Sheraton, announcing that the film, which he intended to call "Finders, Weepers," would be a modern Huckleberry Finn story—although, he reminded the press, "this is another century and the values are different." The Alice *Echo*'s coverage of the news conference ran under the banner headline "HUB CITY HOLLYWOOD."

One place that did not make Santillan welcome in his search for locations was Alice High School. Both Dean and Percy had been suspended for truancy, and the authorities were not looking forward to their return. There had been no serious criminal charges brought against the boys in connection with the Mystery Money. Percy later pleaded guilty to a misdemeanor for the marijuana. Dean was acquitted on the charge of carrying a pistol: in Texas, a bona-fide traveller is permitted to carry a weapon—even a bona-fide traveller who happens to be travelling in the wrong direction. Still, Alice High School had a marijuana problem at the time, and nobody thought that it would be helped by folk heroes who had become famous through suspicious money. As it turned out, there was no need to worry about Dean; he didn't return to Alice. He went straight from Waco to his mother's house—his experience of living with his natural father at an end. Percy was in and out of school for a few weeks after he got back from Waco. The school authorities, who had found him enough of a problem before he started having his picture in the paper, described him to Barrera at one point as "a major disruptive element." Eventually, he went to live with an uncle in California, where he attended school for a few months and then dropped out for good. Dean also had trouble becoming a student again. He tried three or four schools around Corpus; he says the principals tended to complain that his notoriety was a disturbance. "Finally," he said recently, "I just gave up and went to the oil fields." Percy did the same. By the time the trial finally came up, in United States District Court, in Waco—in March of 1981, four years after the bad left turn on Valley Mills Drive—both Dean and Percy were working as roughnecks on rigs drilling for oil and gas in South Texas.

By then, it had been clear for some time that the movie was not going to be released before the trial. A screenplay had been written, and a copy of it had been sent to Alice. Despite Santillan's announcement that the movie would be called "Finders, Weepers," the screenplay told a tale with a happy ending: the boys get the money, Dean decides to go to college, Percy accepts an offer from the New York Yankees for a tryout, and they drive away from the bank in a Rolls-Royce. After a while, though, Santillan was being heard from less and less; eventually, Barrera couldn't find him at all. There had been another development that made Dean and Percy look a bit less like Mark Twain characters, even under the Santillan definition that allowed for different values in different centuries. A year or so after the Mystery Money turned up in Waco, Dean's father, James Hiroms, had been arrested for possession of marijuana with intent to distribute. In November of 1978, he had pleaded guilty and had been sentenced to five years in the federal penitentiary. There was no evidence that the Mystery Money was involved, but no one had much doubt any longer about what kind of money it was. Even after the Hiroms arrest, lawyers for the boys were optimistic. Still, Shaffer and Barrera explored the possibility of making some sort of out-of-court settlement that would divide the money among the boys and the state and, of course, the I.R.S. The state was not interested.

David Bragg and Roy Smithers got involved with the Mystery Money through what lawyers in the white-collar-crime divi-

sion of the Texas attorney general's office referred to as the I.C.B.—
the Interesting Case Bureau. Bragg, a former Peace Corps volun-
teer, and Smithers, a former F.B.I. agent, were part of a group of
high-spirited young attorneys who had gone to work in Austin for
a reformist attorney general named John Hill. They tended to vary
the routine of the caseload now and then with a case that involved,
say, Gypsy scams or a perpetual-motion machine. "We got involved in a lot of wild stuff in the I.C.B.," Bragg said recently. "And
this case fit squarely within the bureau."

Bragg and Smithers figured that they had two tasks. They had
to establish that Dean and Percy knew whose money it was—the
legal principle being, roughly, that if you find a ten-dollar bill on
the ground it's finders keepers but if you saw it drop out of somebody's pocket other rules apply. They also had to rub some of the
Huck Finn mystique off Dean Bridges and Percy Garcia. Bragg
and Smithers shared Barrera's belief that the impression the jurors had of the boys would go a long way toward deciding the ver-
dict. When they thought of the prospective juror they would absolutely have to challenge, they were thinking of the prospective
juror Barrera envisioned as ideal—a middle-aged woman who
seemed motherly. Bragg and Smithers knew how far behind they
were in the public-relations battle when they drove into Waco for
the trial. "We stopped at a filling station," Bragg has said. "And
this man said, 'What in the hell are you doing trying to take the
money away from these poor boys?' We were even greater ogres
than the I.R.S."

When the trial began, before United States District Judge Fred
Shannon, fifteen lawyers were listed as appearing for one side or
another. Before anything else could be decided, there was considerable colloquy about where all of them would sit. It ended with
Shaffer and Barrera and their associates as counsel for the boys
being joined at one table by a rather reluctant ally—the attorney
for the Internal Revenue Service. The I.R.S. man was still making
his discomfort known when he delivered his closing remarks to the
jury ("The United States is not a party to this action because we
believe that Dean Bridges and Percy Garcia are the most deserving

children in the world"), but there was no way to get around the fact that the I.R.S. could get a share of the money only if it went to taxpayers, and the only potential taxpayers in sight were Dean Bridges and Percy Garcia. David Bragg, who sees courtroom strategy as partly a matter of trying to capture the moral high ground, was delighted by the seating arrangement. "There was a great advantage in having the I.R.S. sitting with them," he has said. "Wherever the I.R.S. is present, you get this overwhelming sense of greed."

George Shaffer, a portly man with the courtroom style of an old-fashioned Texas stem-winder, was confident from the start that the boys would get the money. Even before the argument about seating had ended, he summed up his case: "The money belongs to us unless and until the State can show that it does not belong to us. I think that is foregone." The way the state hoped to show this was to demonstrate that the money was not found but stolen: it is a rule of law that title cannot be acquired by theft. Judge Shannon ruled that the search-and-seizure question—the question of whether the police had turned up the money in an illegal search and therefore had to return it to the boys even if it was indeed stolen money—would be argued after the jury had been dismissed. What the jury would be asked to decide was whether Dean Bridges had taken the money even though he knew or believed that its owner could be found. "The essential question," the Judge told the jury, "is whether or not it was found innocently or whether or not the money was stolen."

The case against Dean and Percy was argued mainly by David Bragg—with Roy Smithers vetting the performance and the McLennan County lawyers coming in with a few questions of their own before each witness left the stand. "Our testimony will show that Dean Bridges believes that money to be drug money," Bragg told the jurors. Dean had dug up the money to get back at his father, Bragg said; the trip north was no teenage frolic but Dean's attempt to put as many miles as possible between himself and Alice before the hole in the quail pen was discovered.

If the money was stolen, the attorneys for the boys argued in reply, why hadn't the authorities indicted anyone for stealing it? If it was stolen, whom was it stolen from? Nobody had come forward to claim the money, the lawyers said, and nobody had reported it missing. The boys had found it. Finders keepers.

There was no escaping the fact that Dean's statements about the origin of the cash had been, as his lawyers put it, inconsistent. (The Corpus Christi *Caller* headlined one day of its trial coverage "YOUTH GIVES FOURTH VERSION OF HOW HE FOUND MYSTERY CASH.") According to the lawyers, such inconsistency was understandable in a frightened fifteen-year-old boy who had been questioned relentlessly by police and federal agents. The statement of Dean's that seemed most damaging to his case, though, had been made several months after his interrogation at Waco Police Headquarters—voluntarily and upon advice of counsel. It was a document called a petition for redetermination of deficiency, filed with the United States Tax Court. In that document, which was introduced into evidence by the state, Dean and a certified public accountant representing him attested that the money had been stolen. Why had Dean been advised to make such a statement? The answer seemed to astound even the judge: to get a tax break. An accountant had advised Shaffer that stolen money would be taxed at a lower rate than found money, since it was earned rather than unearned income. At the time the document was filed, Shaffer had been certain that there would be no criminal indictment for theft, since an indictment would have required a victim. He had assumed that a tax document would not be brought into evidence. He had been confident that Dean and Percy were going to keep the money. Why not keep sixty thousand dollars more of it by declaring it as earned income?

The concept had Judge Shannon shaking his head in wonderment. "Am I to understand," he said, "that a fellow who steals money pays less tax on that than a guy who finds the money? You get a tax break for stealing instead of finding? Is that the deal? Is that what the law of this country says?"

"The cases have said if a person is in the business of being a thief that is earned income," the attorney for the I.R.S. replied.

Despite Dean's inconsistencies, he struck Bragg as an effective witness—an obviously unschooled but obviously shrewd young cutup who came across as a rather charming underdog. After the first day of Dean's testimony, in fact, Bragg was pessimistic about being able to change the jury's natural inclination to favor a couple of teen-age boys over the faceless forces of government. Then Dean made an error. He denied that he had ever been arrested on a drug charge in Duval County. Bragg sent a state plane to pick up the record of a marijuana arrest, had the court reporter type up Dean's testimony overnight, and confronted Dean with the disparity in court. At one point, the judge had to give Dean a warning on the penalties for perjury. Dean changed his testimony. For Bragg, the incident helped crystallize the morality play he was trying to stage. "We tried to show through police testimony and the other people we called to testify that those people we normally associate with right and good are all on this side of the case and those we associate with bad are on the other side," he has said. "Once he got on the stand and lied, all these little things fell into place." Dean would presumably disagree with Bragg's characterization of his testimony: when he was asked by Bragg if he had lied in the document sent to the Tax Court, Dean said, "I didn't tell no lie. . . . I just didn't tell the truth."

By then, even Shaffer must have been feeling less confident. His summation to the jury, though, was restrained only in the way that connoisseurs of flowery Texas courtroom performances might define restraint: "He didn't mention the Alamo but once." Shaffer told the jurors that they were the buffer between the power of the government and a simple citizen. "Your destiny, whether it was predetermined millions of years ago or yesterday, your destiny is to sit in this case and be the buffer, the force beyond which the State or the power must go before these two young men, particularly Dean Bridges, may be called, ridiculed, and stated to be a common thief," Shaffer said. "Now, you don't really realize the power of the State until you are up against a large tree or until you are in a rowboat in the middle of the gulf or the bay at the time of a great storm, such as Celia. It is almost like the depth of space. Our mind is not quite big enough to comprehend the largeness, the hugeness of it. It is so powerful that one person cannot over-come it like the storm. You may act as the oars in the storm for these young boys in this particular case. This is a death struggle—no more, no less—between two young men and the power of the State. They are struggling, and their struggle will probably termi-nate today just like it did several years ago with the Alamo."

That's what happened. The jury took an hour and twenty min-utes to return with the finding that the Mystery Money had been stolen. The next day, after hearing more testimony, Judge Shan-non ruled that the money could not be returned to the boys on the ground that it had been illegally seized. He asked for briefs on whether the cash should go to the state or to McLennan County or be split between them. Lawyers for Dean and Percy said they would appeal. Barrera had admired Bragg's courtroom perfor-mance, but he thought the authorities had flimflammed the boys out of the money by reaching what amounted to a criminal ver-dict through a civil case—without having to meet a criminal-case burden of proof or abide by criminal-case rules of evidence. The way George Shaffer put it some time later was this: "They were willing to brand these boys as thieves in order to get their unclean clutches on the money."

A couple of weeks after the trial, a small caravan proceeded down I–35 from Waco to Austin. A delegation from McLen-nan County was going to the capital to talk to state authorities about dividing up the Mystery Money. Briefs would have to be sub-mitted to the court, of course, but the understanding of the lawyers in the case was that the state and the county could work out some sort of settlement and present it in a legal form that would with-stand an appeal. The county judge—an administrative as well as a judicial official in Texas—was in the McLennan County delega-tion, and so were a couple of county commissioners. Two or three people from the McLennan County district attorney's office were along. The meeting was in a large conference room on the seventh floor of the attorney general's office. By then, the attorney general was Mark White, a Baylor graduate, who was already seen as a candidate for governor. White and a couple of his deputies were present. So were David Bragg and Roy Smithers. Bragg and Smithers knew there was going to be trouble, they recalled recently, when the county people began by saying, "Mark, we certainly appreciate the help you gave us in this case." Bragg and Smithers had been under the impression that they had won the case, and won it for the state. It soon became apparent, though, that the money was going to the county.

Bragg and Smithers interpreted the decision as a sort of political pork barrel. The phrases that stick in their minds when they think back on what the McLennan County people said have to do with how badly the folks in McLennan County needed a new jail and how much the folks in McLennan County would like to see Mark White elected governor. The man who was then the county judge interprets the meeting differently. If money is acquired through the criminal-justice system, he says, it seems perfectly reasonable to use it to support the criminal-justice system, and most of the burden of doing that falls on the county—including, as it happened, the necessity around that time of building a new jail to meet a new set of standards imposed by the state. According to a spokesman for Mark White, the decision that McLennan County should get the money was based on such considerations as the fact that the arrest had been made by local rather than state law officers and the expectation that the county could begin making use of the money without waiting the seven-year period required by the escheat law. Whatever the motive for White's decision, it was a matter of policy rather than of law. Bragg and Smithers did not feel they could write briefs that did not strongly support the argument they had already presented in court, and they asked to be removed from the case. Somebody else was assigned to write the briefs. A year later, in early 1982, Judge Shannon awarded all the money to McLennan County.

The lawyers for Dean and Percy thought that their best chance for a reversal by the Fifth Circuit Court of Appeals was on the issue of search and seizure. The Fifth Circuit ruled that the constitutional guarantees against illegal search and seizure were meant to prevent tainted evidence from being used to convict a defendant in a criminal case, and were not relevant in a civil case. The Fifth Circuit's decision was appealed to the Supreme Court, but in February of 1984 the Supreme Court announced that it would not hear the case. Seven years after it began, the legal struggle for the Mystery Money was over. After collecting interest in Waco banks for seven years, the money amounted to eight hundred and sixty-five thousand four hundred and sixty dollars.

Percy Garcia's mother was quoted in the newspaper as saying that she had been praying that Percy wouldn't be getting any of it, because "he is too young and I was afraid that he was going to mess up his life." She said, "If the county needs it more than Percy does, they can have it." ("I saw her praying in the courtroom," Chuck Barrera said when he heard about that comment, "but I thought she was praying for us to win.")

George Shaffer was not feeling as magnanimous as Mrs. Garcia. "I am going to try to find out how McLennan County could steal all that money," he told a reporter, "because in my judgment that is what they did."

Oddly, a lot of people in McLennan County seemed to agree. Given their reputation for straitlaced Baptist morality, residents of Waco might have been expected to approve a decision that a couple of boys who had trouble telling the same story twice could not keep a treasure they had not earned. Given the normal complaints about the taxpayer's burden, McLennan County taxpayers might have been expected to rejoice at the news that an extra nine hundred thousand dollars had been thrown into the county's kitty. But every time the case was prominently mentioned in the Waco *Tribune-Herald* half a dozen citizens sent in angry letters accusing the county of having stolen the money from the boys. Nobody has ever written a letter to the editor on the other side. Instead of being thanked for having captured the money for the county on a long shot, county officials have been accused of bullying and "the most hideous attitude of petty jealousy." After the Supreme Court decision, a *Tribune-Herald* editorial that supported the county's actions as perfectly proper acknowledged that "the critics who have called county officials thieves over the past six years won't stop just because the highest court in the land decided that the money was indeed ill-gotten." The editorialist was correct. In Waco, most people still seem to think that if anyone connected with the Mystery Money did any stealing it was their own county government. As it turned out, Chuck Barrera's strategy of establishing the boys in the public mind as Huck Finn and Tom Sawyer worked even without the movie—failing to impress only the jurors who heard the evidence in court.

M ark White is now the governor of Texas. David Bragg and Roy Smithers are partners in a private law firm in Austin; on the wall of Bragg's office is a framed newspaper clipping with the headline "HUCK FINN TALE ENDS FOR TEENS." George Shaffer still practices law in Corpus Christi, and Chuck Barrera still practices law in Alice. When Barrera was asked not long ago what he got out of the case, he said, "The ice chest." Somehow, it ended up on his porch. Thinking back on the case, Barrera says that it turned on the arrest of Hiroms ("It was dirty money then, and they couldn't let the boys have it; they just had to figure out a legal reason") and the introduction of Dean's statement to the I.R.S. about having stolen the money—a statement Barrera had not known about until shortly before the trial. "It turned out to be real good tax planning," one of Barrera's law partners said recently. "They didn't have to pay a nickel in taxes."

Nobody in Alice writes angry letters to the newspaper complaining that the boys should have been allowed to keep the money. People in Alice are more inclined to say something like "These boys were not the sweet little boys next door." The surprising fact that McLennan County ended up with the money did cause a few people to wonder why Jim Wells County didn't make a claim. The South Texas approach to judging motives being what it is, that sort of speculation turns inevitably to trying to figure out who had the most to gain if the county stayed out of the case. Actually, lawyers familiar with the legal struggle over the Mystery Money don't think that a serious argument could have been made for Jim Wells County. Someone in Alice who is told this may shift to speculating about who owns those banks in Waco that were allowed to hold all that money for all those years.

There is still a chance for Hub City Hollywood. Just after the Supreme Court decision, Barrera got another call from the Coast. The MGM/UA Entertainment Company expressed interest in the movie rights to the boys' stories. Since Santillan's option had expired, the rights were available. If the movie is shot, the boys stand to make about twenty-five thousand dollars each. As of now, counting the Santillan option money and the MGM/UA option money, each has made only a few thousand dollars more than Dean gave his friend John Rose that evening for a ride to the bus station. Rose was not required to hand over four thousand dollars to McLennan County, but the county was awarded just about everything else. "I didn't know they'd leave me with nothing," Dean said recently. "Not even the clothes, not even the car." The Thunderbird has been driven from government storage in San Antonio to Waco, where the county will sell it at auction. The boys are supposed to get their Sears bluejeans back, but Percy, who has put on some weight since he was a sixteen-year-old baseball player, says that they wouldn't fit anyway.

Dean and Percy are, of course, no longer boys. Both of them do a man's work on the oil rigs. Both of them are fathers. Both of them live in the sort of tiny rental bungalows that have Masonite panelling on the walls, and toys on the floor, and a television set turned on as long as anybody is awake. Dean has a mustache now; Percy has a beard. Right up to the end, they were confident that they would get at least part of the money. Even now, when people in the oil field ask them if they're going to get it they are not quite willing to say, "No, never." They talk sometimes of some other lawsuit, or maybe some other lawyers. Still, they have begun to talk about the money in the past tense. Percy says he regrets not having noticed a flashy Hilton nearby before he and Dean checked into the slightly frayed Baker. "I ain't never going to have that kind of money again," Dean said recently. "I'd be doing good just to buy me a house. It ain't going to be early retirement for me." Dean says that when he drove that blue Thunderbird onto the interstate he figured he would just travel all his life. "I didn't think I could spend it all," he says. "I didn't get to spend hardly any of it."

—1984

BAD LANGUAGE

When I read that the young Ross Perot's stated reason for wanting a hardship discharge before he had fulfilled his naval obligation was that sailors were always "taking God's name in vain" and behaving promiscuously on shore leave, I had to wonder whether he knew a lot less about the Navy when he was in high school than I did.

While I was growing up—in Kansas City, Missouri, just a couple of states and a few years from Perot—we were aware that sailors did not always behave absolutely respectably, particularly in foreign ports. That was part of the draw. In fact, if I had been asked to explain the traditional appeal of the Navy for the sons of the Midwest in two words, I believe those two words would have been "shore leave." We were desperately envious of shore leave. We didn't even have any shore.

We also liked the idea of all that cussing. These days, of course, it's common to hear grannies talk dirty. But when Ross and I were growing up, talking dirty in front of grownups was certainly frowned on—or maybe swatted at would be a better way to put it— and talking dirty in front of girls wasn't done much either. The Navy, we thought, offered a young man from the Midwest the opportunity to cuss all he wanted.

Lest you think the notion of sailors regularly taking the Lord's name in vain was strictly a product of our fevered teenage imaginations, I should point out that our parents reinforced this view by occasionally referring to some respectable-looking older citizen as having the capacity to "swear like a sailor."

All of which makes it surprising that Ross Perot applied to the Naval Academy under the impression that he could get through there and through the active duty the Navy expected in return for his free education without hearing any strong language. I can only assume that the phrase "swears like a sailor" wasn't heard much in

Texarkana, Texas, during the time he was growing up there. It may be that Kansas City was a more worldly place than Texarkana; if so, though, how do you explain the fact that at Hale H. Cook grade school in Kansas City I went through the entire Second World War under the impression that Japanese people had yellow blood?

In Texarkana, young Ross may not have had enough contact with sailors to know whether they cussed or not. In the movies of those days, a sailor who dropped a forty-pound shell on his foot would have never said anything stronger than "Dang-nap it."

Even so, you'd think that someone in his senior high school class—some worldly fellow who had transferred in from, say, Amarillo—could have predicted the "moral emptiness" of Navy life that Ross described with such shock in the letter his father forwarded to the congressman who had appointed Ross to Annapolis and to both Texas senators. But it's possible that as a high school student Perot simply brushed aside the warning.

"Ross," I can imagine the new boy in town saying, "I know you have your heart set on going to Annapolis, but I have to warn you that serving in the Navy could mean being in close proximity to people who take the name of the Lord in vain on a fairly regular basis."

"There's not one iota of truth in that," young Ross says, having already acquired some of the straight-from-the-shoulder bluster that the American voters will one day love. "If you can show me one example of that, I'll buy milkshakes for the entire class."

The boy from Amarillo, still determined to warn Ross of what might lie ahead, says that, from what he is given to understand, sailors on shore leave sometimes engage in acts with complete strangers that the Lord meant only married people to do with each other, and then only if they promise not to talk about it.

"Stuff and nonsense," young Ross says. "Not true. And I have a dozen members of the senior class who are willing to swear that it's not true. I don't have to sit here and listen to some slick Amarillo guy in alligator shoes try to trip me up."

The new boy from Amarillo starts to say he is, in fact, wearing penny-loafers, but young Ross is launched on a lecture. "If there is swearing in the Navy, the way I'll take care of it won't be pretty, but you'll never hear any of it again, I can tell you that ..."

"O.K., Ross," the boy from Amarillo finally says. "Have it your way."

—1992

SCOUTING SLEEPERS

About a year ago, I decided to become a book scout for Marcia Carter and Larry McMurtry, because they made it sound so easy. They are partners in a Georgetown rare-book shop called Booked Up—a name whose origins I have, as a gesture of friendship, not investigated. A scout in the rare-book business is what the antique trade would call a picker. Looking for books that he can sell to a dealer, a scout will work over the shelf at, say, the St. Joseph's Ladies' Auxiliary Thrift Shop, confident that what the other browsers take to be a dusty old industrial pamphlet he will recognize as the first published book of Thomas Wolfe. A book scout will scout garage sales and antique stores and charity book sales. He may even scout rare-book shops; it is axiomatic in the trade that nobody can know everything about books, and a dealer with an awesome knowledge of poetry and Americana might be harboring an enormously valuable nautical work that he had been planning to include in the next batch of books donated to the local Veterans Administration hospital. I had never thought of becoming an antique picker. It's a perfectly legitimate way of making a living, but the word suggests a small, gnarled man poking through rubbish heaps. Being a scout sounds adventurous; McMurtry regards it as "a form of sport." It occurred to me that someone who travels as much as I do could be a book scout on the side, in the way an anthropologist who studies Indians may work up a small sideline in silver jewelry. McMurtry used to make his living as a book scout. He has been known to say that he is the best book scout in the country; he once tried to arrange a sort of *mano a mano* with a West Coast scout at a charity book sale in Des Moines. For a number of years, of course, he has made his living as a writer—mostly a writer of novels set in Texas, where he grew up. A book scout would consider him a successful novelist, since a mint-condition first edition of his first novel, "Horseman, Pass

By," would fetch about a hundred and twenty-five dollars. Mc-
Murtry, to his mild displeasure, once even ran across a stack of
his own letters for sale at a stiff price. When I heard the story, my
displeasure was acute: I realized that after answering the only letter I could remember receiving from McMurtry—a nicely typed,
unstained document containing a discussion of Midwestern barbecue which a certain sort of literary critic might find of interest—
I threw it away.

Writers are not ordinarily book collectors. I know a few writers who have large libraries of what people in the rare-book trade
would call, with some condescension, "reading copies"—books
that are of sufficiently modest value to be read without fear that the
odd coffee stain might drastically reduce the owner's net assets—
but McMurtry is the only American writer I know of who has developed a professional interest in rare books. McMurtry says that
when he first began collecting books, as a student at North Texas
State College, in the fifties, he must have done so on the assumption that anyone who was apt to go back to a home town like Ar-
cher City, Texas—the town used for filming McMurtry's novel
"The Last Picture Show"—had better own any book he might ever
want to read. These days, after having accumulated and sold two
or three libraries, McMurtry owns mostly reading copies himself,
except for some small and eccentric collections like books on the
Yellow Peril and books on Siberian travel. Owning a bookshop, he
says, "cools the fever" of collecting. Owning a bookshop has also
drastically cut down on McMurtry's scouting—book dealers like
to stay in their shops, on the theory that, as they often say, "anything might walk through the door"—but his scouting fever has not
cooled. He compares book scouting to cowboying, acknowledging
in the process that he was a fairly miserable cowboy. His father,
McMurtry says, could spot a cow he wanted and return the next
day to cut it out of a herd of two thousand; to Larry all cows looked
alike. Not books. Larry knows which shade of blue cover on a copy
of "Native Son" indicates a first printing and which one doesn't;
he knows the precise value of poetry books by Robert Lowell that
Robert Lowell may now have forgotten writing. Dealers normally

do not show up at the large charity book sales; scrambling around with a horde of laymen among thousands of books is not their style. But McMurtry has often been first in line at the book sale held annually in Washington to raise funds for Vassar—a position that can reflect a willingness to camp on the sidewalk the night before the sale.

When I decided to enrich myself in the book trade, McMurtry and Marcia Carter gave me a short course in how various publishers identify first editions—a course I forgot so swiftly that I was able to phone excitedly a few weeks later to report finding an extraordinary first edition published by a firm that Larry identified for me as strictly a reprint house. The next time I phoned, I was in Charleston, South Carolina, where I had just grabbed a first edition of William Faulkner's "The Hamlet" for a quarter at an event that I remember as a Huguenot Society bake sale. Marcia answered the phone. Marcia spent the late fifties at the Madeira School and Vassar instead of at North Texas State College. A stranger who wandered into Booked Up under the impression that a female book dealer is a stout, gray-haired woman whose cigarette ash is about to fall into a book by Thomas Carlyle might mistake her for a customer who has dashed in to pick up a leather-bound book of nineteenth-century poetry to take to the hostess of a particularly smart Georgetown dinner party; in fact, Marcia would have probably had to refuse the dinner party to attend a book auction in Baltimore, and her gifts are normally more antic than leather-bound poetry, the most notable one to Larry having been a sweatshirt that said on it "Minor Regional Novelist."

She seemed pleased to hear that I had found a first edition of "The Hamlet." "How nice!" she said. "With a dust wrapper?"

"Well, no, not exactly," I said. "No dust wrapper."

"Oh," she said. "Well, it's a nice book anyway."

"If you must know," I said, "page 8 is taped, and, as long as we're being absolutely honest, so is page 9, owing to its proximity to page 8. It's sort of dirty. I'll keep looking."

I kept looking. I didn't pay high prices. My father—who started buying books in his retirement, mostly at garage sales—told me once that he never paid more than a dime for a book unless it was something special. Allowing for inflation, I am my father's son. With a quarter here and fifty cents there, though, I figured I had made some shrewd buys. We agreed that I would bring my haul to Washington this spring during the Vassar book sale—giving me a chance to see McMurtry operate as a scout at the same time. I lugged about fifteen books from New York to Washington with me—the only scout on the shuttle.

L arry had decided that we would have to spend the night on the sidewalk to guarantee being first in line, and Marcia cheerfully agreed to participate to the extent of lending me a pillow. Marcia does not scout the Vassar sale; she is on the other side. Even before she went into the rare-book business, she worked on the sale as what she calls "one of the moles"—the Vassar alumnae who work through the year pricing and categorizing the books that have been donated. Volunteers like Marcia try to limit the number of books that would qualify as what scouts like Larry call sleepers—books that, through carelessness or ignorance, have been priced with the herd of popular novels and book-club editions instead of being cut out for special attention. As part of her temporary role of adversary rather than partner, Marcia further harasses Larry by doing an imitation of what he sounds like while trying to get the first grab at the cardboard boxes full of books brought by volunteers to restock the tables after the first rush. ("Can I help you with that, Ma'am?")

At ten-thirty, we arrived at the site of the sale—the ground floor of a nearly completed office building—and found it free of lurking book collectors. McMurtry threw an empty Army duffel-bag on the sidewalk next to the door and sat down. It had been a couple of years since McMurtry was the earliest arrival—last year he didn't wander in until almost daybreak—and he seemed happy to have regained his primacy. When a tall man carrying a sleeping bag showed up around eleven-thirty, McMurtry said, "Well, Shannon, you're late." Shannon, a computer operator, collects mainly illustrated books and nostalgia; in past years he had been accompanied by his son, a Charlie Chan collector. As it turns out, most of the people who regularly show up early to wait in line are specialists, who dash off in different directions once the door opens. McMurtry, being the only regular whose main interest in front position is having first crack at the rare-book room, says he could actually do as well by being fifth or sixth in line instead of first—except, of course, for the honor. At the Vassar sale, the books of obvious value are displayed in a special section, with its own checkout counter, and it is McMurtry's custom to head there on a dead run. A couple of the Vassar alumnae in charge of the sale—women Marcia introduces as the queen moles—have been working on it for more than twenty years, time enough to have acquired what even the scouts acknowledge is a nearly professional grasp of the field. But, the point of their operation being to dispose of a hundred thousand books during the five days of the sale, they tend to mark even non-sleepers at a price that is well below what might be encountered at a dealer's. When the door opened, at ten the next morning, McMurtry was almost certain to be the first customer into the rare-book section, carrying his empty duffelbag. We would not, it turned out, be forced to spend every minute of the intervening eleven and a half hours on the sidewalk; for the past few years a collector of Lincoln books who is always among the early arrivals has taken it upon himself to hand out numbers that allow people in line to go for a stroll or even leave for breakfast without losing their places. The Lincoln collector showed up about midnight. "Hey, George, you're a little late this year," McMurtry said in greeting. Armed with our numbers, we decided we would have breakfast around seven at my hotel—giving McMurtry the opportunity to get a preliminary glance at the bagful of sleepers I had brought from New York.

M cMurtry lined up the books on the dresser of my hotel room. "I would say that some of them are worth twenty-five cents and some of them are worth fifty cents," he said.

"That's what I paid for them!" I said.

"Well, you didn't lose any money," he said.

I told him I wanted a formal appraisal by both partners of the store—not a quick glance by someone who was obviously suffering the effects of having spent the night dozing on the sidewalk. On the way back to reoccupy our places in line, I said, "What about that first edition of 'The Caine Mutiny'?"

"It isn't a first edition," Larry said.

"Nobody likes a niggler," I told him.

An hour before the door opened, all one hundred and twenty of the numbers the Lincoln collector made had been handed out. Larry introduced me to some collectors back in the line—including William Matheson, the rare-book librarian at the Library of Congress, and his wife, Nina, also a librarian, who is known among rare-book people in Washington not only as a collector of H. G. Wells and Nabokov but as someone who has a particularly sharp eye for a sleeper. At the Vassar sale the previous year, she had paid fifty cents for a copy of "The Cocktail Party" that was signed by T. S. Eliot. A few minutes before the door was scheduled to open, while McMurtry was back in our assigned spot doing something like fluffing up his duffelbag, Matheson mentioned that a Canadian colleague had, during a recent visit to Washington, perused the stock of Booked Up and selected, for ten dollars, a copy of "Maria Chapdelaine," by a French-Canadian writer named Louis Hémon. The book, Matheson's colleague had told him, was worth eight hundred dollars. "I don't know whether to tell Larry or not," Matheson said. Everyone urged full disclosure as the only honest course. McMurtry rejoined the group and was told about Louis Hémon. He managed what I believe the novelists call a weak smile, and mumbled something about living and learning. A scout scouted. I considered telling him that I had never heard of Louis Hémon, either; I also considered telling him that Louis Hémon had always been my favorite French-Canadian novelist. Then someone said we had better take our places in line.

At ten o'clock, McMurtry burst through the door of the Vassar book sale. He dashed past a table full of old magazines, skirted the Mystery table, and skidded to a halt in the section that had been partitioned off as the rare-book room. There were eight or ten tables within the rare-book section; McMurtry started right to work on one that had been labelled "Treasure Table." He began snatching up books and tossing the ones he wanted into his duffel-bag—making the decision with the sort of quick confirming glance a housewife working the canned-soup section of the supermarket uses to make sure she has picked up cream of tomato rather than tomato with rice. Only a few seconds after ten, McMurtry already had what he believed to be the two most valuable books on the Treasure Table—an eighteenth-century manuscript cookbook and a copy of William Godwin's essay on population which the author had inscribed to a friend. He quickly finished the Treasure Table and, still in the rare-book section, headed for tables marked "First Editions" and "Art and Architecture." By the time he reached the Rare Americana table, he was dragging a heavy duffelbag behind him. Suddenly he rolled the duffel shut, slid it far under the Rare Civil War table, and dashed past the rare-book checkout into the general section empty-handed. "Never stop to pay out of the rare-book room right away," he had told me just before the door opened. "It's a death trap." McMurtry, carrying two paper shopping bags he had picked up somewhere, was now working the rest of the sale—finished, for the time being, with rare books. It was two minutes after ten.

The huge room began to fill up with people carrying shopping bags and cardboard boxes and even pushing grocery carts. McMurtry made a quick pass at the Poetry counter, spent a couple of minutes at Short Stories, and headed for Fiction, where he figures there are always opportunities for sleepers—particularly in writers of the Harlem renaissance and American radical fiction and a category that people in the trade call "minor moderns." One of his shopping bags was already full. I could see a jam-up of people trying to check out of the rare-book section. McMurtry worked his way down the Fiction table—occasionally snatching up a book and tossing it into the shopping bag or, after flicking open the cover, putting it back on the table. People were still pouring through the door, and there was some jostling at the tables as customers tried to reach for books while holding an armful they wanted to consider. At ten-thirty, McMurtry stashed his two shopping bags, both full, against a pillar and threw his coat over them, planning to cull them later in the afternoon. Then he went out for a Coke.

The next morning, when Larry and Marcia met me at my hotel for breakfast, he seemed moderately satisfied with his haul. He often does better on the second day of the sale, he said, when the crowd has thinned out and the tables are gradually refilled from the stock in the back room or the books that other buyers have, upon consideration, decided to leave behind. McMurtry figured the cookbook, which had cost seventy-five dollars, was worth two or three hundred and would be bought immediately, cookbooks being a very hot item in the rare-book business. He had also picked up a dime rehearsal copy of some Tennessee Williams one-act plays which he had reason to believe was rare and valuable, after putting back on the Treasure Table a thirty-five-dollar first edition of Williams short stories, because it had not turned out to be in pristine condition. Nina Matheson, to no one's surprise, had paid fifty cents for a first edition of John Barth's first novel, "The Floating Opera"—a book worth about seventy-five dollars. I thought it was an appropriate time to show the two partners my books, so we went up to my room for a thorough inspection.

"They do have a certain uniformity of condition," Larry said, taking a better look than he had managed in his sleepy state the previous morning.

"Yes," Marcia said brightly. "Drab to spotty."

I handed Marcia a copy of a travel book I had bought for its illustrations, pointing out that it had a rather attractive dust wrapper.

"I've never seen the Literary Guild edition of 'Hot Countries,'" she said, in the tone the boss's wife might use to say to her young hostess, "My, I've never had bologna as an appetizer before."

Larry said my copy of "The Hamlet" was what book people call lightly foxed—speckled with brown spots—and was further defaced by the stamp of the Travis Rental Library.

"Take a look at these two Steinbeck novels," I said.

"Late and common," Larry said, as if discussing the last family admitted into the country club.

"And 'The Caine Mutiny'?" I asked.

"An astute dealer might be able to get a dollar and a half for it," he said. "Maybe three or four for the Faulkner."

"I'm taking the Faulkner home with me," I said. "I might even read it."

"Why don't you leave the rest of these in a lower drawer here?" Larry suggested.

"I couldn't do that," I said.

"Well, there's one thing you could do with them," Marcia said.

"I know," I said. "I'm donating them to the Vassar book sale."

—**1976**

CONFESSIONS OF A SPEECHWRITER

"Ｂut didn't you once work as a campaign-speechwriter yourself?" I was asked, after I'd observed that writing campaign speeches is to writing what making mud-pies is to cooking.

Well, yes, I did work as a speechwriter many years ago. The way I prefer to put it is that I wrote speeches for the last successful Democratic peace candidate—Lyndon B. Johnson. At the time, President Johnson was running against Sen. Barry Goldwater—someone the president accused of being reckless enough to consider sending American boys to fight a ground war in Southeast Asia.

There was very little chance that I would be one of the boys Senator Goldwater had in mind—I had finished my Army service a few years before—but I figured that the only way to make absolutely certain was to defeat Goldwater and thereby prevent the United States from getting seriously involved in Vietnam. I hired on with LBJ at the White House (actually, the Executive Office Building, next door), he won in a landslide and the rest is history—the sort of history you get if you pay any attention to campaign promises.

And were my speeches any better than the ones I've denigrated? Not on your life. They were at least as bad, and maybe worse. They contained the cheap applause lines and the lame jokes. Their use of numbers was what you might call imaginative. When I'm questioned closely at the pearly gates about the writing I did in the 1964 presidential campaign, my only defense will be that, as far as I was able to tell, President Johnson didn't use so much as a sentence of it, and I am therefore not responsible in any way for the war in Vietnam.

Did I write lies? We don't like to use that word. Let's just say that when you hear a number in a campaign speech, about the best you can hope for is a distortion rather than an out and out whop-

per. When I heard George Bush, in his acceptance speech at the
Republican National Convention, say that Bill Clinton had raised
taxes and fees 128 times as governor of Arkansas, I murmured, "I
wonder whether they counted the time the parking meters in Fay-
etteville went from a dime to a quarter."

Apparently they didn't, but it was close. For instance, they
actually did count a 1987 law that lengthened the Arkansas dog-
racing season, on the theory that an extended season brought in
more money from the state gambling tax. I'm not sure that my
counting methods were quite that imaginative, but, asked to defend some of the numbers I put in speeches, I think I would retreat
to my basic defense that the president didn't use the speeches
anyway.

Often, he would just set them aside and ramble on in what we
called his county commissioner speech—speechifying in, say,
Pickens, South Carolina, about how his grandpaw passed through
Pickens in nineteen and thirty, and about how the local Pickens
congressman was the one ole boy who could just walk into the
Oval Office and get what he wanted, and about how Barry Goldwater didn't even know anybody in Pickens.

Sometimes, some poll result or some desperate cry from a Democratic congressional candidate would cause a sudden schedule
shift that made the speech prepared for that day irrelevant. The
president, scheduled at the last minute for a farm bureau audience in Iowa, would have no use for the exquisite overview of ur-
ban problems I had composed for what was supposed to have been
a campaign stop in Newark.

The speech I worked hardest on was for a campaign stop in
Utah. After considerable research, I wrote a speech about the
American spirit of discovery and expansion, using the second
great trek of the Mormons—the one to St. George, Utah—as an example. I incorporated historical accounts that described the extraordinary courage of Mormon pioneers who, resisting the temptation to settle for the comparative comfort of what had become
Salt Lake City, pushed once more into unknown territory to build

a new temple at St. George. It was, I thought, my finest speech, and I was absurdly optimistic that the president would use it.

Then the man who was in charge of our small coven of speechwriters walked into my office and announced the president would be going to Philadelphia rather than Salt Lake City.

"Just cross out 'Mormons' everywhere you see it and write in 'Quakers,'" I said.

He didn't think that would work out. I don't remember what happened after that, except that I must have written an entirely different speech for Philadelphia. I assume that the president didn't use it. I assume that there were a lot of numbers in it.

—1992

AND ESPECIALLY TO PICKENS, S.C.

A document recently unearthed

I can't tell you good people how good and full my heart feels to be in Pickens.

You know, my great grandfather was from Georgia, and he never went through Pickens.

In fact, as far as we know, Pickens is the only town in the continental United States he didn't go through, although we hadn't realized he went through the District of Columbia until some research just before this election.

So you can see that the people of Pickens and the people of Texas have always been very close.

I wish Lady Bird had come with me today. Because sometimes, just in the privacy of our own room late at night, I whisper to Lady Bird, "You know, I love the people of Pickens . . .

". . . and they love me."

You know, in this task that God has thrust upon me, sometimes I leave the House in the morning, and kiss Lady Bird and Luci Baines and that other one good-bye, and I don't know if I'll see them again that night.

Because they might be at a rally at Culpeper or the Brooklyn Navy Yard or Yazoo City.

Places where my great grandfather passed through.

I feel at home here in Pickens, especially with my old friend B.Q. Jeffries here on the platform with me. Because B.Q., let me tell you, knows how to get things from me for Pickens, and when he strolls into that oval office and tells me something, I say, "B.Q., how is it you're the one man in Congress who can just stroll into this oval office and get me to do anything you want? What is it you have on me anyway, B.Q.?"

Well, B.Q. doesn't have anything on me, of course, except that we've been pals since about Nineteen and Thirty, when I used to go to B.Q.'s ranch and swap old Texas stories—fertilizer stories and sheep jokes and all those good old farm stories that you and I understand and hold so dear.

And what would I do without Orville Scroggins?

Barry Goldwater doesn't even know Orville Scroggins.

Orville Scroggins is the one Senator in Washington who—let me tell you—who can just get me to do anything he wants. He just comes strollin' into that oval office and tells me what the good people of this state need, and I say, "Orville, why is it you're the one man in Congress who can get me to do anything you want for those folks."

Folks, I'm just so glad to be here, and see all your happy, smiling, desperate faces, and let you touch my hand that I just don't know what to say through this bull mike.

Except that your President loves you.

Every last little bitty one of you.

You know it's true.

And I know it's true.

And the people of America know it's true.

See the people of America know it's true.

They know it's true.

Run, people, run.

They have a dog.

His name is Spot.

See Spot run.

Run, Spot, run.

Well, as I was saying, I'm not going to indulge in name-calling with that raving, ranting demagogue.

You know what Barry Goldwater has ever done for Pickens?

Not a goddamned thing.

I want to keep this campaign on the level it belongs, so let's get to the great issues of our time.

Under this Administration, we have built six sluice dams in Pickens—eight if you count the Greater Pickens Metropolitan Area.

We have given thirty-two F.H.A. loans, most of them not repaid.

And a $31,000 National Guard budget, including a brand new four-wheel-drive jeep.

Orville Scroggins knew you'd love that four-wheel drive.

And the Republicans?

Under Warren Harding, the time he was President, the Republicans closed an agricultural feed station here in 1921.

Are those the kind of people you want to entrust the lives of four billion people to?

The stakes are big.

And the answer to that is No.

You say No.

I say No.

All God's chillun say No.

See God's chillun.

They say No.

Run, chillun, run.

Well, let me tell you that Pickens will never be forgotten under this Administration.

When the tax cut is fully effective, twenty-eight jobs will be added in Pickens.

All Federal jobs.

I love those twenty-eight jobs. I love those people. I love that tax cut.

Because a long time ago, when I was a boy on that poor, scrubby, lonely, run-down farm (list value: $4.85, without outbuildings), the one I grew up on down in Texas, I was walking under the Texas stars, just thinking, and lucky for me, Dick Goodwin was walking alongside of me taking down everything I thought. There we were, walking along like soldiers in a minefield, like you do on a farm, and I thought maybe some day I would be President of the most powerful nation in the history of the earth—thank God—and I would go to my people and I would *tell* them how many jobs they would get when the tax cut becomes fully effective in their area, and I would *teach* them how much a bushel of soybeans would cost if price supports were dropped (which is a suggestion my opponent made in a moment of weakness and we get a lot of statistics out of), and I would open my heart to them and tell the American people that their obsolete air base would not be closed as long as Lyndon Baines Johnson is the monarch of this great land.

And that is what we mean when we talk about the Great Society.

Do you want to repeal the present and veto the future and hold our guard up and our hand out and tell a man to go to hell and not make him go there, with Sam Rayburn standing right in the room?

The answer to that is:

No.

Me neither.

What we want is a Great Society, where everybody's just as happy as a turkey on the day after Thanksgiving and loves each other and God and me, and the old are young and the young are in Vietnam.

That's what we mean by the Great Society.

So don't choose the radical who would take away everything you have and don't deserve.

This Administration represents the mainstream of the calm, sensible policy of Franklin Roosevelt and Harry Truman and Dwight D. Eisenhower and John F. Kennedy. It is the policy of Arthur Vandenberg and Woodrow Wilson and Everett McKinley Dirksen and Everett McKinley and Glen Taylor and Warren Harding and Eric Haas and Connie Mack and Innocent III and Emanuel Celler and James Eastland and Vito Marcantonio. It is the policy of Dean Acheson and Dean Rusk and Dean Sayre and Pierre Poujade and Claude Pepper and Jomo Kenyatta and John Connally and John Nance Garner and Jeremy Bentham and Adam Smith and Adam Yarmolinsky and Eve Arden and Deanna Durbin and Turhan Bey.

It is my policy.

This Tuesday, the American people will go to the polls and give an historic mandate for *that* policy.

You know, late at night, in that big white house, behind those big black gates that they keep locked and chained, I sit in that oval office, after all the work of the day has ended, and after I've given Orville Scroggins and B.Q. Jeffries every last thing the good people of Pickens can use, and I look at my desk and I look at the moon and I get close to my God and I try to think just what we do mean by the Great Society.

And you know it.

And I know it.

And John knows it.

And Mary knows it.

See John run.

He must know it.

—1964

KNOWING JOHNNY JENKINS

On the weekends, Robert Donnell likes to take the country roads. He's in no hurry. During the week, he has a stressful job—he works on the Texas Gulf Coast, supervising the switching of freight cars at the port of Beaumont—and his idea of how to refresh himself during his free time is simple: "Put it in neutral. Don't pay nothin' no mind." When he travels between Beaumont and Austin, where his children live with his ex-wife, he often finds himself on Farm-to-Market 969, which cuts through rich pastureland along the Colorado River east of Austin. It's a peaceful stretch of road; in the springtime, its shoulders are often covered with bluebonnets. On a beautiful Sunday afternoon last April, driving back to Beaumont after watching his son play in a Little League game, Donnell got off 969 to give his dog some exercise and take a stretch himself. This was at a public boat ramp below a bridge in Bastrop County, about thirty miles from Austin. The Colorado River, which determines the shape of downtown Austin, continues from the capital all the way through Bastrop County on its way to the Gulf. Donnell often stopped at that boat ramp. He had lived in Bastrop County for a while, and he had often gone tubing down the Colorado until, in the building frenzy of the Texas boom in the seventies, the pollution from Austin sewage made the Colorado the sort of place you wouldn't want to float around in.

There was a time when 969 crossed the Colorado by way of a rickety old contraption known locally as Humpback Bridge, but a few years ago Humpback Bridge was replaced with a proper steel-and-concrete structure that has no name. Underneath it, there's a patch of concrete that includes not just a boat ramp but also some stairs going down the bank to the river, and a sign about the sort of safety check that should be made on any boat before it's put in the water, and a trash can, and even a picnic table, for people who don't mind having a picnic that's punctuated every so often by the rumble of a car overhead. The banks in both directions are thick with willows and cottonwoods. The Colorado is wide there, and rather murky—although, as a sort of silver lining to the bust that followed the seventies boom, there's less pollution than there once was. The water moves slowly, in a way that can sometimes be perilously deceiving to a swimmer who doesn't know about the undercurrents. The boat ramp under what was once Humpback Bridge is a sylvan spot, but not exactly remote. There is no other public boat ramp between Bastrop and Austin. The sheriff of Bastrop County, Con Keirsey, says, "People put their boats in there. People go down there to make love or sell dope or picnic—recreate." Sheriff Keirsey's deputies are in the habit of dropping by when they're in the area, just to make sure that none of those activities have got out of hand.

When Donnell got down to the boat ramp, he noticed another car, parked parallel to the river—a gold Mercedes, with the passenger-side door open and the left-rear tire flat. Next to the Mercedes was a wallet—empty except, as it turned out, for a Social Security card. Explaining later why he didn't just finish his stretch and move on, Donnell said that he's from a family with deep roots in Texas law enforcement. In fact, his uncle, Nig Hoskins, served as the sheriff of Bastrop County for years before Con Keirsey took office. Donnell stopped at the county seat—a pleasant old trading town, also called Bastrop, that is only a few miles from the boat ramp—and turned in the wallet at the sheriff's office. The dispatcher sent a deputy named Jim Burnett out to the boat ramp to have a look. When Burnett arrived, the Mercedes was still there, and so were three fishermen. As he spoke to them, one of them was casting down the river, and, in an eddy where a thick willow limb dipped into the water, his hook snagged on something. It was a shirt. Caught up against the willow limb, just a few feet from shore, was a body. The cause of death was immediately apparent: a large-calibre-bullet wound in the back of the head.

The victim, it turned out, was the owner of the car and the wallet—John H. Jenkins III, a forty-nine-year-old rare-book dealer from Austin. Some of his friends said later that the drama involved in the discovery of his body was, in a sad way, appropriate, because Johnny Jenkins had always had a flair for the dramatic. Jenkins' supporters and detractors in the rare-book business agreed that he simply loved publicity. His death was front-page news not only because of the violent circumstances but also because he had often been on the front page when he was alive. After Robert Donnell happened upon the gold Mercedes at the boat ramp in Bastrop County, the Austin *American-Statesman* ran a story on John Jenkins that was headlined "BOOK DEALER'S LIFE READ LIKE A BESTSELLER." A piece on Jenkins by one of the paper's columnists carried the headline "WORD WILDCATTER LEAVES LEGEND."

The legend was built partly on John Jenkins' being a bookdealer of such broad interests that he could be known both as the author of the standard bibliography of Texana, "Basic Texas Books," and as a poker player good enough to compete in the World Series of Poker, in Las Vegas, under the sobriquet Austin Squatty. There were standard highlights of the legend told whenever Jenkins hit the papers, and they were brought out on the occasion of his death: the story of how even before graduating from high school he found and edited and annotated the pioneer reminiscences of his great-great-grandfather and published them in a book that carried an introduction by the renowned Texas man of letters J. Frank Dobie; the story of how he sold his childhood coin collection to finance a round-the-world honeymoon; the story of how he rose from modest beginnings to become an internationally known bookdealer and the president of the Antiquarian Booksellers Association of America; the story of how he worked with the Federal Bureau of Investigation to ensnare some thieves who had brought him an Audubon folio stolen from Union College, in 1971; the story of how, in 1975, he bought the single greatest supply of Western Americana right out from under the noses of the Easterners and carted it back to Texas, trailing in his wake a gaggle of Yankee booksellers panting to get their hands on his treasure.

There were some disquieting stories, too, in those newspaper articles. John Jenkins was a man whose premises had been the scene of at least three fires, the last of which, in 1987, was ruled arson by the police. He was a man who had sold—innocently, he insisted—a large portion of some Texas Revolution letters and broadsides that began to circulate in the early seventies and were only last year, in a revelation that shocked the Texas rare-book world, demonstrated to be forgeries. He was a man who in recent years had experienced some serious business reversals unconnected to the book business—a disastrous oil-rig operation, for instance, and an equally disastrous attempt to turn an abandoned college campus into a conference center, and a feature horror film called "Mongrel," which may not have been in release even long enough for some smart-aleck movie critic to talk about what a dog it was. "I suppose he was a man who lived two lives," an old acquaintance in Austin said after the body of Jenkins was found. "Or maybe three."

There had been a time when the Jenkins Company was a sight to behold. This was in the late seventies, a few years after John Jenkins became a kind of instant star in the rare-book business by buying the stock of the Eberstadt brothers—dealers in Americana who had gradually withdrawn from the marketplace—in what may have been the largest rare-book transaction to that date. From the outside, the Jenkins Company didn't look like any rare-book shop that anybody had ever seen; it was a huge yellow corrugated-aluminum structure on the service road of I-35, just south of Austin. Jenkins had originally bought the building to use as a warehouse for his publishing enterprises—a company that did mostly reprints of books relevant to Texas history, and a vanity press that did books relevant only to the people who paid to have them published—but he had also moved his book business in after a 1969 fire in his store downtown. He always referred to the I-35 building as "the plant." Someone who entered the plant in those days expecting the sort of décor that might be customary in a warehouse on the service road of an interstate was in for a shock. A kind of entry hall had been constructed. Its floors were parquet. Its walls were old apothecary shelves lined with leather-bound volumes. There was a vast Oriental rug. There was a Victorian set-tee. There were prints and old Western broadsides and framed articles that mentioned John H. Jenkins III.

Even beyond the entry hall, the plant had surprises—the sort of wagon that was pulled by an eighteen-mule team, for instance, and a room-size safe that the insurance company had required for the Eberstadt books and, of course, the office of the proprietor. Jerry Conn, a writer and teacher in Austin who knew Jenkins from Beaumont, where they both grew up, says he realized as soon as he entered that office that he was not dealing with the Johnny Jenkins he remembered—"a skinny little weeny kid with glasses." Conn was at the Jenkins Company to discuss the publication as a book of an expanded master's thesis on Preston Smith, widely considered the least colorful Texas governor of modern times until Dolph Briscoe came along. "It's sort of dark back there where you are when you come in," Conn said recently, recalling what it had been like to enter the office. "And you go up to this huge desk. It's like Dorothy and the Scarecrow and them going up to the Wizard of Oz." And there, behind the huge desk, in a massive, magnificently ugly chair that amounted to a menagerie of gargoyles, was Johnny Jenkins.

Jenkins was a small man physically—he may have been five feet six- and his build suggested someone who had spent his childhood collecting coins rather than playing football. His office, though, reflected a strong attraction to the outsize scale associated with Texas. To Conn, it was as if Jenkins had consciously adopted a character, and the character was the brash Texas wheeler-dealer. When Jenkins was outside Texas, he was costumed for the role. At a book fair in Chicago or New York or London, he was likely to show up wearing a Stetson and cowboy boots—accoutrements he ordinarily didn't bother with in Austin—and smoking a huge cigar. To some booksellers, the effect was like coming across a toy Texan. People in the trade still remember Jenkins' performance at a New York book fair in the late seventies. He had rented a large suite at the Plaza, and he invited a number of colleagues up for a poker game. There was a big bowl of shrimp—so big that it was said to have cost fifteen hundred dollars. The poker game would not have been particularly high-stakes. Ray Walton, a semi-retired Austin bookdealer who was a longtime friend and admirer of Jenkins, has said, "A poker game to John—what it was was an audience." At the table, Jenkins would sit cross-legged, the way Indians in movies sit around the campfire—a habit that was later cited as an explanation for the name Austin Squatty. In his storytelling mode, he also had a customary pose—hands in his back pockets, cigar rolling around from one side of his mouth to the other. And if someone said that the story being told didn't sound like the precise truth Jenkins might say, "O.K. Let's see hands. How many want a good story and how many want the truth?"

Beaumont, an oil-refining town a few miles from the Louisiana line, is not the sort of Texas place that immediately conjures up cowboy boots, but Jenkins always identified more with Bastrop County, where both sides of his family had come from. In fact, his widow told authorities, he had presumably been in the area of the boat ramp on that Sunday in April searching for a grave marker as part of his research for a book on Edward Burleson, a Bastrop hero of the Texas Revolution—a figure who had interested Jenkins ever since he was a child, when he used to spend his summers among a swarm of grandchildren his mother's parents presided over in Bastrop. "Even then, the thing that was impressive to everybody about him was his intensity," one of his cousins, a minister in Bastrop named Ken Kesselus, has said. "He wanted to excel. He hated to waste time. He wanted to do something with his life. When the other boys were figuring out how to steal watermelons, he was working on a book or starting a coin collection." From the start, Johnny Jenkins, skinny little weeny kid or not, was a go-getter, a self-improver, a mind-stretcher. J. P. Bryan, a second-generation collector of Texana who lives in Houston, met Jenkins when they were both University of Texas students interested in the Texas State Historical Association, and through the years, as a friend and occasional business partner and constant customer, he never lost his amazement at Jenkins' energy. Thinking back on Jenkins recently, Bryan said, "He was one of the few people I've ever known who could sit in a chair and seem to be moving."

Before Jenkins left the university, he had established a shop in downtown Austin for his coins. He handled some books in the shop, too, and scouted around for books to sell to rare-book dealers. He was, as he had been since childhood, ready to trade anything for anything. Summing up his business career after his death, Maureen Jenkins, his widow, said, "John was basically a horse trader." Trading is a natural extension of the rare-book business; dealers often buy estates and find themselves with any number of items that would look odd on the shelves of a bookstore. In Texas, which has an honored pioneer tradition of haggling and bartering, trading among people who dealt in books and antiques evolved during the sixties into a phenomenon that nearly qualified as a spectator sport. At the center of the game was Dorman David, a dashing young man who had family money and a remarkable eye and a taste for the high life and, fairly regularly, a short-term cash-flow problem. David remembers one trade this way: "One time, I took a mummy to Waco, Texas. It was in a coffin— a sarcophagus of carved wood. That was a big trade. I got Travis letters from the Alamo, probably Bowie knives, and some guns. I may have got a log cabin." In a *Texas Monthly* piece last spring on the Texas forgeries, Gregory Curtis mentions a number of sixties trades, including one in which "Jenkins got a Rolls-Royce, a Kentucky rifle, and a Bowie knife; Price Daniel, Jr., the son of the former governor and a bookdealer before he became a politician, got a book collection; a car dealer who had owned the Rolls got an antique racing car; a restaurant owner got several thousand Cuban cigars; and David got a $20,000 credit at Maxim's in Houston, which he traded for some rare wines, which he in turn traded to Jenkins for books and documents." Memories can be fuzzy on such oral agreements, and one version of that trade includes two tickets to a Dallas Cowboys game.

There is no disagreement about John Jenkins' skill as a trader. He was smart, of course—the sort of person whose friends often described him as having "an I.Q. that's out of sight." There were

stories about how he could spell any word or speak five minutes
on any historical question. ("You couldn't stump him. If he didn't
know it, he could make it up and make it sound like he knew it.")
He had a confident way of discussing subjects you wouldn't think
he knew anything about. And he had brass. "When he made a deal,
he'd want one extra thing," Cookie Baumel, a poker friend who often traded with Jenkins, has said. "If he'd traded you a car dealer-
ship, he would have said, right at the end, 'And, oh, I want a car at
cost for the next so many years.' He was a good dealer. He knew
how to do a deal where everybody felt good about it." Some people,
though, see the fabled trading of the sixties as simply a device—one
among many—for transferring whatever was accumulated by the
tasteful and imaginative Dorman David to the wily John Jenkins.
The novelist Larry McMurtry, a Texan who has been involved in
the rare-book business all his adult life, sees the relationship that
way, and he sees Jenkins as having acquired something more than
books and prints and Texas broadsides from Dorman David: his
flamboyance, his dash, his color. In McMurtry's view, "John Jenkins sort of came out from under Dorman David."

Dorman David readily admits that in those days he was a "wild
boy"—someone who went from escapades and excesses to a bad
heroin habit and, eventually, a jail term. His father, Henry David, was sometimes known as the mud king of Texas—a tough
man who had started with nothing and made a fortune in what is
known as drilling mud. The David family sounds like the stuff of a
Texas novel, and McMurtry, who once worked at the Bookman, the
store founded by Dorman David, sometimes sounds as if he might
be sketching it out as he speaks. Henry David was apparently not
always pleased at the idea of his family's spending his mud money
on elegant furnishings and exotic plants and the stock and fixtures
of what many considered the single most beautiful bookstore in
the country. In McMurtry's recollection of those days in the late
sixties, the comings and goings of various family members during domestic storms of one sort or another were so intense that
one small moving company in Houston did virtually nothing but
move the Davids. Of all the Davids, Dorman cut the widest swath

through Texas, leaving a trail of wrecked cars and sunken pleasure craft and splintered marriages. Recently, he recalled that during those years he was married four or five times and involved in a couple of relationships that were in effect marriages. ("I guess I was just following my heart.") Among bookdealers, Dorman David was known as a horse trader who often ended up without any horses—a man who usually paid too much for an item he simply had to have, and then, when pressed, had to sell it or trade it for too little, often to John Jenkins.

For a while, Jenkins and Dorman David were among the partners in an Austin gallery that specialized in Western art. In the early years, Jenkins had J. P. Bryan as a partner in his publishing operations. But the center of Jenkins' commercial life was always the rare-book business. At a certain level, the rare-book business is to a great extent a mail-order business, conducted as often as not with other dealers, and Jenkins gradually built up his catalogues and his stock, concentrating on Texana. He cultivated customers—often, in his case, institutions. He bought collections and tried to figure out what to do with what couldn't be sold. By all accounts, he loved buying books, and he loved all the more buying books of great size in large lots. "He'd say, 'I'm here to buy some big fat books,' as a sort of joke," Bill Reese, a New Haven specialist in Americana, has said. "But then he really would buy a lot of big fat books." Jenkins often referred to himself as "the world's largest bookdealer." In a business associated with meticulous men carefully examining one item at a time, Jenkins had an abiding interest in quantity; in a business sometimes noted for its quiet politesse, Jenkins, whose closest friends acknowledge that he had "an ego the size of Texas," was interested in making a splash. William Simpson, a Houston auctioneer of antiques who often traded printed material to Jenkins for manuscripts ("Houston is a manuscript town"), normally speaks in the orotund tones and ornate phrases common to his calling, but he once summed up a lot about John Jenkins' behavior in one short sentence: "He needed to be noticed."

Jenkins did not make an immediate splash in the rare-book

trade, but he did build his business. Using a computer before many of his colleagues had made the conversion, he churned out a lot of catalogues. In the early years of his business—the years of Democratic Administrations pushing federal aid to education, and of great university expansion to accommodate the baby boom—university libraries all over the country tended to have healthy acquisition budgets for rare books. Among rich Texans there was an increasing interest in acquiring Texana—and there was an increasing supply of rich Texans. When Lowdermilk's, a Washington bookstore noted for its supply of government publications, had a closing sale, in the early seventies, John Jenkins was the big buyer. The huge corrugated building on I-35 began filling up with books. Then, in 1975, Jenkins bought out the Eberstadts. In the words of his old friend J. P. Bryan, "The reflected glory of that transaction put him in a different atmosphere."

What is usually spoken of as the Eberstadt Collection was not, in reality, a collection but simply the inventory of Charles and Lindley Eberstadt, brothers who, succeeding their father, had become the country's preeminent dealers in Americana—the only dealers certain wealthy collectors and rare-book libraries would buy from. As they grew older, the Eberstadt brothers had begun a gradual slide from hard-to-deal-with to semi-retired, and by 1969 they had moved what remained of their stock from premises on Madison Avenue to Montclair, New Jersey. By the time Charles Eberstadt died, in 1974, it had been so long since anybody had been given a good look at the inventory that no Americana dealer could claim to have a reliable notion of what was in it. Jenkins had cultivated Lindley Eberstadt for years. When it appeared that Lindley was prepared to sell out, for a variety of tax and estate reasons, Jenkins, putting together financing from an old Texas friend and some Wall Street investment bankers, managed to buy the Eberstadt stock for what was probably around two million seven hundred thousand dollars—a staggering sum in the rare-book trade in 1975. The purchase consisted of forty thousand items, some of them one-of-a-kind books or pamphlets whose existence dealers had not been aware of. According to Michael Ginsberg, a Massachusetts bookdealer who was present for some of the negotiations, "Johnny said, 'Until 1975, Eberstadt was the market. Now I'm the market. Now everybody has to come to Texas.'" With Ginsberg's help, Jenkins had the booty loaded into a rental truck and hauled to the corrugated-aluminum building on I-35.

The Texana had been spoken for by the University of Texas—in fact, U.T.'s agreement in advance to buy that part of the stock, for what turned out to be about a million and a half dollars, was one of the elements that had made the deal possible—but the rest of the books were for sale almost as soon as they were out of the trucks. Dealers, two or three at a time, came to Austin from all over the country. They would wander through the books, make a pile of what interested them, as they might at the annual used-book sale to benefit the scholarship fund, and then have the books priced by Jenkins or Mike Ginsberg. Jenkins tended to have the dealers met at the Austin airport, sometimes by a Cadillac—this was Texas, after all—and he entertained them at lavish dinners. He said that bringing the Eberstadt books to Texas was part of a cultural shift toward Texas which he had always dreamed about. Several years later, he explained to a newspaper in Beaumont that the dominant role played in American cultural life by Philadelphia in the eighteenth century and Boston in the nineteenth and New York in the twentieth would be played by Texas in the twenty-first.

Oddly, nobody is certain how well Jenkins came out on the Eberstadt books. There is no question that, profit aside, the coup of the purchase provided the splash that made him a major figure in the rare-book business. From 1975 to around 1982, the period that is generally accepted in the trade as John Jenkins' heyday, the Jenkins Company was a professionally staffed operation that did a few million dollars' worth of business a year, partly on the momentum or the actual books of the Eberstadt purchase. But whether the Jenkins Company in fact made a substantial profit from those forty thousand items is a different matter. Jenkins, pricing piles of books in those first weeks after the purchase, told everyone that the pressure he faced was seven hundred dollars a day in interest charges. Some bookdealers believe, though, that once he had nailed down the University of Texas payment to cover a good part of the loan he could have stopped for a while to make a more systematic study of what his stock was worth. ("I don't think anybody knew Texana better than Johnny," one dealer has said, "but outside Texana he was shooting in the dark.") On the other hand, they tend to acknowledge that the man who had the prudence to do that would probably not be the man who had the brass to grab the Eberstadt books in the first place. John Jenkins loved to sell books even more than he loved to buy them. "Whenever John had something good, he had a fever in his brain to turn it over," Bill Reese has said. "If you got there when he was trying to get his nut back, you could get some tremendous deals. He was in a fever to turn that Eberstadt stuff."

Jenkins often offered reporters an estimate of what the Eberstadt stock was "worth"—a word that bookdealers tend to treat with the sort of suspicion they might direct at a browser who seems to be lingering for a long time next to the first editions and is carrying a voluminous shopping bag. But the figure was constantly changing, and, as it happened, nobody in the book business, friend or foe, took figures tossed out by John Jenkins very seriously anyway. When Jenkins, a man enamored of sheer quantity, told a reporter how many books the Jenkins Company owned or how much they were worth, one Austin bookdealer has said, the safe course was always to take the square root of the number mentioned. The numbers—the number of trucks that had been required to bring the books he bought from Lowdermilk's back from Washington, say, or the number of pre-1835 newspapers he had in stock—invariably grew larger, because everything about a Jenkins exploit grew in the retelling. (Even the first version could be of a size not immediately recognizable to those who had been at the scene. Larry McMurtry insists that he picked up a Texas newspaper after the most serious fire at the Jenkins Company, on Christmas Eve of 1985, and saw the headline "RARE BOOK LOSS TERMED GLOBAL DISASTER.") Over the years, colleagues watched the story of how Jenkins turned in the Audubon-folio

thieves swell from a fairly straightforward bust after a meeting
at a motel—an incident already interesting enough to have drawn
an inquiry from the producers of the "Kojak" show—to a bullet-
sprayed, blood-spattered adventure so gripping that it was in fact
the basis for an episode of "Kojak." When Jenkins wrote a sort
of memoir called "Audubon and Other Capers," his inscription
in a copy for Kenneth Rendell, a prominent autograph dealer he
had known for years, said, "The whole truth, and nothing but the
truth—as I remember it."

In the words of a bookdealer who didn't like him, Jenkins was
"indifferent to the truth." Those who did like him—people like his
old friend Ray Walton—would not say that he was indifferent to
it, but they would acknowledge that he never claimed to prefer
it to a good story. Walton, for one, never saw anything sinister in
that. "No matter what coup, no matter what recognition he got,
it wouldn't be enough recognition unless he made it a little big-
ger," Walton said recently. "John learned at an early age that most
reporters are lazy and gullible and wrote down anything he told
them. So gradually he began stretching. I think he got the Eberstadt books up to twenty million dollars at some point. But most
of those enhancements were harmless. He didn't use them to
swindle people. He was just feeding his ego. It was all a hilarious
game to him. It was almost that he felt like it was his duty to make
it a little more entertaining."

Exaggeration was natural to the character of a brash Texan who
did things in a big way. Some people in the trade were offended
by the character and by Jenkins' single-mindedness in trying to
create it. "I thought he was a caricature of himself," a Texan who
used to work at the University of Texas library said not long ago,
recalling her embarrassment when the Grolier Club, an organization of New York bibliophiles, took a tour of Texas and Jenkins
forced the bus driver to make a detour so he could show everyone
his grand house. "Everything he did, from getting a book or catch-
ing the Audubon thieves, he milked so relentlessly," she said. "The
image of who he was became all-consuming." People who admired John Jenkins and people who didn't admire him agree that

he was, in effect, a self-legendizer. "His image in the public—he lived for that," Dorman David said shortly after Jenkins died. "For him to be 'a fabulous person' was more important than anything else to him."

Admirers and detractors also had differing interpretations of the same facts when it came to the way Jenkins ran his business. There is no doubt that, compared with other bookdealers of his prominence, Jenkins sold through his catalogue a significant percentage of books that were what bookmen call "not as described." Rare-book dealers use the word "collating" to mean going through a book page by page when it arrives to make certain that it is complete, and, in the words of one Austin dealer, "you never collated a book from John Jenkins only once." Jenkins once bought what is called the hospital of an English bookstore—the collection of hurt and incomplete books that is kept partly as what amounts to a repository of spare parts—and some of the incomplete books apparently found their way into Jenkins Company catalogues without a full accounting of quite how incomplete they were. In most catalogues, the abbreviation "fxd" means that a book is foxed—that it bears brownish stains caused by oxidation. In a Jenkins catalogue, it meant "foxed, general wear," and someone not familiar with the Jenkins usage could find himself with a book in need of hospitalization. "His shortcomings as a rare bookseller were well known, and by and large discounted by his colleagues," Ed Maggs, who worked briefly for the Jenkins Company, wrote in a sympathetic obituary of Jenkins. "It was once suggested that his catalogues should bear the legend that all books should be considered defective unless otherwise stated." Whether the surprising condition of many of the books sent out by the Jenkins Company was the result of carelessness or of deceit depended on what the recipient thought of the proprietor. There were people in the trade who believed that Jenkins had the sort of business practices that "might do in the coin business," or even that he was a simple crook. Some other people thought that Jenkins was merely, as one of his friends put it, "not one for details." Those holding either view agree that Jenkins' response to having an incomplete or damaged book returned was to refund the purchase price cheerfully and perhaps make a joke or two about it.

In the opinion of his longtime friend J. P. Bryan, some of Jenkins' sloppiness about business matters came from impatience. "He did everything as if he was off to catch the subway," Bryan has said. At times, though, he put in hours at a stretch cataloguing books—a lonely and exacting task—and his bitterest enemies acknowledge that "Basic Texas Books" is an impressive piece of research that will probably be the standard bibliography of Texana for the foreseeable future. Even at that, though, he was impatient. He sent the galleys to New Haven to be read by Bill Reese and Terry Halladay, who now works with Reese but used to be at the Jenkins Company. The two of them went over the galleys carefully and sent them back with any number of comments—not only stylistic suggestions but factual corrections. Jenkins sent them an effusive note thanking them for their trouble, but the book contained none of their corrections. Reese thought it was typical Jenkins: "He really wanted to be right, but he was probably in a hurry to get it out."

"The funds are here, and where you find money you eventually find culture also," Jenkins told the Houston *Chronicle* at the time of the Eberstadt purchase. He said that the oil-and-gas wealth of Texas was "apparently permanent wealth," and went on, "Everything seems to be dead or dying in the East, but it is just beginning here." As things turned out, of course, Texas oil-and-gas wealth was not even semi-permanent. Seven or eight years after the Eberstadt purchase, the entire state seemed to be going broke. At around the same time, the best years of the Jenkins Company were coming to an end, and there are people in the trade who would say that one phenomenon explains the other—that John Jenkins just rode up and down on the Texas economy. Jenkins, that theory goes, began to prosper when the Texas boom was creating a new generation of rich Texana collectors and when the Humanities Research Center, the principal rare-book repository at the University of Texas, was a "bibliovacuum-cleaner," buying so many books every year that there wasn't time to confirm the presence of all the pages. It's true that Jenkins sold fairly regularly to the Humanities Research Center in the seventies, even though its collection consists of literature rather than Texana or Americana, but he was not one of its major sources. It's also true that there were some Texans who went from being collectors in the boom to dodging collection agencies in the bust, and that acquisition budgets of large university libraries across the country tended to decline in the eighties. But the rare-book business at the level Jenkins was engaged in it had become a national, or even international, business long ago; an operation the size of the Jenkins Company could not have prospered or failed on the basis of Texas buyers alone.

There was a central element of the Jenkins Company's business that did depend on the condition of the Texas economy—credit. It took some years for Texas bookmen to convince Texas bankers that rare books should be acceptable as collateral. Some of Jenkins' colleagues thought that the Jenkins Company kept its entrance hall lined with so many handsomely bound sets—the rich-looking but not particularly valuable editions that book people call "leather" or "furniture"—to impress bankers who could never have been persuaded that the real money was in some faded pamphlet. When banks finally did begin lending money on books, John Jenkins, a renowned juggler of loans, apparently passed up few opportunities to borrow. During the boom days, banks seemed to open at about the same rate as shopping centers, and, in the recollection of someone who worked at the Jenkins Company in those years, "every time a bank opened, Johnny went down and took out a loan." That sort of financing ended abruptly when banks in Texas began to fail in large numbers. These days, an Austin businessman who goes down to his local bank in search of a loan is less likely to encounter the old acquaintance with whom he last talked at the Kiwanis barbecue than a rather remote administrator for the Federal Deposit Insurance Corporation who has been too busy calling in overdue notes to attend such gatherings. It is said in Austin that what a Texas bank now wants to see as collateral for a hundred-thousand-dollar loan is a hundred-thousand-dollar certificate of deposit right there in the same bank.

Nobody claimed that John Jenkins—a man who sometimes seemed to crave action more than profit—was a careful businessman. "The one thing Johnny could never get through his head was the economics of the business—the price of cataloguing books and housing books, for instance," his friend Mike Ginsberg has said. "He thought if you bought a book for fifty dollars and sold it for two hundred you made a hundred and fifty dollars." And nobody claimed that Jenkins was a man determined to live within his means. Still, a lot of people in the trade say that he would have done just fine, even in a soft economy, if he had only been able to stick to the book business. "If Johnny had wanted to focus his full attention on the book business, he would have been the greatest bookdealer in the United States," J. P. Bryan said recently. "It wasn't lack of talent. It was lack of focus." It may be true that what finally crippled Jenkins financially was the drain of his outside disasters at a time when he didn't have the stock or the credit or the focus to recoup his loss in the book business. In a way, though, saying that John Jenkins should have confined himself to a business he had mastered is like saying that he should have been more painstaking in the way he priced and sold the Eberstadt books: it's true, but it's almost the equivalent of saying that he should have been a different person. People who knew Jenkins always speak about his enormous energy, his need for challenges, his almost desperate need to be noticed; some of them say that after the jolt of the Eberstadt sale subsided, in the early eighties, Jenkins seemed bored by the book business. Not long ago, someone who had known Jenkins in Austin outside the book trade said that he might have found himself better suited to the life led in the Texas pioneer era that so fascinated him: what with trying to get some land cleared and a house built while holding off the Indians and putting in some crops, he might have used up all that energy. Living in more modern times, he was always looking for something.

His friends saw poker as simply another outlet for Jenkins' energy and his need for challenge—or, as one of them put it, "an opportunity to show that he was smarter than everyone else." His detractors saw it as compulsive gambling. When he began going to Las Vegas, it was as a blackjack player. He had taken a course in card counting—he had a head for numbers and, like most book-men, a first-rate memory—and, according to some of the people who used to accompany him to Vegas in those days, he got good enough at keeping track of the cards to be banned at some casinos. Jenkins had been playing poker since he was a boy in Beaumont, and he had presided over a weekly game in Austin for years. In the late seventies, the weekly game gradually became more serious and more expensive. Jenkins began devouring books on poker. He began playing in some out-of-town games, and he started competing in Las Vegas. He won several trophies, which he displayed at his house; he acquired a flashy jacket, emblazoned with "Austin Squatty," which he seemed to take particular pleasure in wearing at rare-book events. He may also have lost a lot of money. There are people who think that Jenkins was draining money from his business years ago to pay gambling losses, but there are also people who remember his saying years ago that he had saved his business more than once through poker playing. His friends don't claim to know the truth. "When Johnny came back from Las Vegas, he always said he'd won," one of them has recalled. "But he would have said that anyway."

In the mid-eighties, Jenkins was still as likely as ever to show up in a magazine spread describing himself as the largest anti-quarian bookdealer in the world, but the gap between the numbers he tossed off and reality was steadily increasing. As the years wore on, he became less and less a factor in the rare-book business. Most of the professional staff that he had built up after the Eberstadt sale drifted away. The catalogues, which had once come pouring out of the computer in Austin, came out less often and seemed to list a lot of books that had been in the previous catalogues. Dealers who dropped in to see what Jenkins happened to have on hand had increasing difficulty finding books to buy from the Jenkins Company. In the late eighties, an Austin bookdealer has said, Jenkins seemed to be getting to the point at which the best way to describe his position in the book trade was with the old Texas phrase "all hat and no cattle."

Whether the fire that destroyed a good deal of the plant on Christmas Eve of 1985 was a serious blow to the fortunes of the Jenkins Company as well as a global disaster or whether it was—as some cynics in the trade would maintain—a short-term solution to some of John Jenkins' cash-flow problems is still the stuff of late-night conversations at book fairs. "It cut the legs right out from under us," Michael Parrish, the manager of the Jenkins Company, has said, maintaining that the insurance settlement, of three and a half million dollars, went basically for bank notes and that a number of valuable books were outside the fireproof room that had been installed for the Eberstadt stock. Other people in the book trade have described what was lost that Christmas Eve as "a bunch of remainders" or have described the fire as "the best sale Johnny ever had." The Christmas Eve fire was ruled accidental, but a fire in September of 1987 at the building that Jenkins was using during the rebuilding of the plant was ruled arson—with no conclusion reached as to who had committed the arson. The settlement paid to Jenkins for the Christmas Eve fire, also known as "the big fire," had a terrible effect on the premiums of other bookdealers. And, in an industry that had previously experienced fires so rarely that some dealers couldn't think of one offhand, the fact that John Jenkins had enough fires to require identifying subtitles for them had a terrible effect on his reputation.

One bookseller who had particular reason to be disenchanted by the 1987 fire was Jennifer Larson, of San Francisco, who was hired by Jenkins' insurance carrier to make an appraisal of the Jenkins Company stock. She arrived in Austin thinking of John Jenkins as one of the leaders of the business ("in Western Americana No. 1, without question"), but she came to believe that some of the items she was judging "could be demonstrated to be not genuine." In looking around for counsel, she found that Tom Taylor, an Austin bookseller and printer, was already involved in a painstaking investigation of Texas forgeries. Taylor's research had begun when he was told about a copy of the Texas Declaration of Independence by a printer who suspected its authenticity. The conversation made him focus on a thought he had never really permitted to come to the surface of his mind: that some important documents of the Texas Republic period, including original copies of the Texas Declaration of Independence, seemed to be a lot more common than they had once been. "Every time I walked into a library, another one seemed to pop up," Taylor said. "You have the feeling in the pit of your stomach that something is wrong."

Taylor began tracking them down, looking for their provenance, and subjecting them to scrutiny. What he found was astounding simply in numbers alone. Until 1973, for instance, there had been two known copies of a broadside printed from the "Victory or Death" letter that William Travis wrote at the Alamo; Taylor tracked down twelve more. Over roughly the same time span, extant copies of the Texas Declaration of Independence had gone from five to twenty-one. The copies that had not been around before the seventies, Taylor's examinations showed, were fakes. He found fakes in many of the most distinguished rare-book libraries of Texas; he found that a Texas Declaration of Independence owned by Governor Bill Clements was a fake. Of the thirty-six fake documents whose provenance he could trace with certainty, Taylor later wrote, the ownership trail of all of them ended at one of three places. Five had been sold by Dorman David, nine by William Simpson, the antiques auctioneer in Houston, and twenty-two by the Jenkins Company—"including at least 6 copies of the Travis letter and 4 copies of the Declaration of Independence." None of the questionable documents sold by the Jenkins Company had been sold publicly, through a catalogue—a fact that some people in the trade found even more suspicious than the sheer number of documents involved. Jennifer Larson has said, "You'd think that if a man like John Jenkins had a document like that he'd put it on his Christmas card."

Dorman David acknowledges that he made the plates that were presumably used for at least some of the forgeries. His intention, he has said, was to do a folio of facsimiles of important documents having to do with the settlement of Texas. He says that the plates were in some boxes of material he sold Jenkins and Simpson when, broke and hooked on heroin, he finally got out of the book business forever, in the early seventies. Jenkins and Simpson both denied that they had acquired any plates or forgeries from David. Simpson, who had always dealt in rare books and documents simply as supplementary lots in auctions dominated by ornate European furniture ("You want everything on the menu"), said he had acquired most of the questionable documents he sold from Jenkins—a position that lent a certain symmetry to the inquiry, since Jenkins said that many of his were from Simpson. In a letter circulated to Texas booksellers last fall Jenkins said of David, "I have no accusations to make against him and personally believe that whatever misbehavior if any he was ever engaged in, he paid the price with the loss of his business and reputation, the frying of his brain and loss of his health, and with serving a term in jail." Jenkins pointed out that virtually every rare-book dealer in Texas had sold one of the fake documents at one time or another; Taylor himself had sold four. It was no wonder that the Jenkins Company handled more of such documents than anyone else, he wrote in his letter, since "during the past two decades, the Jenkins Company has been by far the largest dealer in Texana, our sales being in excess of $30 million dollars in books during that period."

There are people who think that John Jenkins was by nature so optimistic that he could have sold four copies of the Texas Declaration of Independence without wondering why there were suddenly so many, but those people are a minority. Jenkins was after all the country's leading authority on Texana—not to speak of being the security officer of the Antiquarian Booksellers Association of America. Among the theories spun out by book people about the forgeries, the best case normally put forward for Jenkins is that, like a number of other dealers who were making a good profit on Texas documents, he had what Tom Taylor once referred to as "a need not to know." The worst case is that he found a stack of documents in the material he had bought from Dorman David, or was actually involved in creating the fakes. The truth would probably not have emerged even if Jenkins had lived.

Questions of who knew what when are not easily answered beyond a reasonable doubt, and, once some passes at restitution had
been made, the institutions involved were not inclined to pursue
the matter. No criminal indictments were brought. The A.B.A.A.
did rather abruptly organize a security committee to replace its security officer, and after some prodding by a few members it established a questioned-imprints committee to make a sort of inventory of forged documents and turn it over to the ethics committee.
But this spring, a year after Taylor's findings first made news in
Texas, the ethics committee had just received the inventory and
was beginning its inquiry into whether any A.B.A.A. member had
knowingly sold a forgery or had not given proper restitution when
something he sold turned out to be a forgery. Meanwhile, one Austin bookdealer said recently, "Johnny was left to the rumor mill."
In the book trade, a small community whose members are in constant contact, the rumor mill has always had a high rate of produc-
tivity. The people in the book business who hadn't had much use
for Jenkins to begin with—people who were offended by his manner or suspicious of his business methods or, close friends of his
would say, envious of his flashy and much publicized leap to the
top of the field—saw both the 1987 fire and the forgery scandal as
confirming what they had been saying about him all along.

By this spring, Jenkins found himself wounded by rumors and
beset by financial troubles that were quite concrete. He was being sued by the F.D.I.C. for a million-three-hundred-thousand-
dollar loan obtained in connection with the drilling-rig operation.
Because of his failure to keep up payments on a six-hundred-
thousand-dollar loan, an Austin bank had given notice that it
would foreclose on the I-35 building, and a date had been set for an
auction on the steps of the Travis County courthouse. "He tended
to think he could overcome problems," J. P. Bryan has said of Jenkins. "But I will say that he had some overwhelming problems."
He had apparently told some close friends that he might have to
start over again, but, they say, he gave no indication that the prospect of doing that had put much of a dent in his native optimism.
In fact, those close to Jenkins insist that he was in a particularly

jovial mood on that Sunday in April. His cousin Ken Kesselus was his collaborator on the book about Edward Burleson, and he has said that Jenkins was "like a kid" at the prospect of finishing up the revisions and publishing a biography of a historical character who had interested him since his childhood. According to Kesselus, Jenkins, the sort of historian who likes to pace up and down the field where the battle took place, had reason to believe that he finally knew where Burleson's father was buried, and was itching to drive out to Bastrop and have a look.

I n those first days after Robert Donnell's discovery at the boat ramp in Bastrop County, the circumstances of John Jenkins' life led naturally to speculation about the circumstances of his death. There were people who assumed that Jenkins had been trailed to Bastrop County and murdered because of something having to do with gambling—murdered by mobsters because of a gambling debt, perhaps, or by a gambler he had caught cheating. There were people who thought that he had been the victim of random violence at the hands of thugs who had been attracted by the roll of bills and the Rolex watch he customarily had on his person. There were people who figured that the thieves caught in the Audubon heist might have finally got out of prison and taken their revenge. There were even people who thought that Jenkins might have been killed because of something having to do with the Texas forgeries, although nobody could think of quite what. There were also people who believed that John Jenkins had committed suicide. Foremost among them was Con Keirsey, the sheriff of Bastrop County.

Although Sheriff Keirsey is a former Austin homicide detective, he fits the popular picture of a rural Texas sheriff. He wears a proper sheriff's outfit: a hand-tooled leather belt with "Con" imprinted on the back and a buckle with a bull on it fastened on the front; cowboy boots; Western-cut pants; a Western shirt with pearl buttons; a straw hat in the traditional Stetson cut; and a star. He looks something like a larger, thicker version of Audie Murphy, and he talks the way Murphy talked, in one of those slow Southwestern accents that make the speaker sound as if he's having trouble getting his mouth completely around the words. He even says the same sort of things Audie Murphy might say if he were playing a sheriff, like "I've been doing this for thirty years. I might not be the best at it, but I know a little." Sheriff Keirsey acknowledged that at first glance it appeared that John Jenkins had been murdered. His money and his credit cards were missing, and so was his Rolex—a President model, which is said to be so popular among gamblers in Las Vegas that it has an established price in any pawnshop. No note had been left. Jenkins had been shot in the back of the head—an unusual place for someone who wanted to do himself in to aim. Most important, the sheriff had been unable to find the gun, even though more shoreline had been exposed by holding the river at a hydropower station upstream and divers, using metal detectors and a powerful magnet borrowed from a nearby Air Force base, had pulled from the water an assortment of objects that included hand tools and silverware and auto parts and golf clubs and the keys to Jenkins' Mercedes and, astonishingly, someone else's Rolex.

There were, in other words, any number of reasons to conclude that Jenkins had been murdered. But the sheriff said that it was all too pat. To him the crime scene and the bullet trajectory and the multitude of problems that had beset Jenkins all pointed away from murder. According to Kesselus, Sheriff Keirsey was inclined to view Jenkins' death as a suicide the day the body was found, and that inclination was apparently strengthened when, only a few days later, the sheriff spoke to some people who said they had been present when Jenkins discussed, hypothetically, ways in which it might be possible to rig a suicide to make it appear to be murder—a discussion that concentrated on methods of separating the gun from the body. For whatever reason, Sheriff Keirsey seemed to be taking the position, early in the investigation, that Jenkins had killed himself in a way designed to make his death look like a homicide.

Jenkins' family and his closest friends were outraged by the sheriff's theory. They disagreed with his reading of the physical evidence, and they disagreed with his analysis of the problems that Jenkins was facing. Jenkins was certainly in a spot, his friends say, but think of how many spots he had been in before. He was known as a man who somehow always managed to land on his feet. Financial problems just as bad were facing a lot of people in Austin who did not necessarily have Jenkins' resilience. The bankruptcy rate among the top ten developers in Austin, for instance, now stands at a hundred per cent. "Johnny had plenty of company," Ray Walton told the *American-Statesman.* "If all the people who got foreclosed on in Austin killed themselves, the corpses would be piled up like cordwood." Jenkins' lawyer insisted that there was no financial incentive for Jenkins to fake a murder—no suicide clause or double-indemnity clause in his insurance policies, for instance. J. P. Bryan has said that he and other friends of Jenkins' had been meeting with some success in trying to restructure some of his outstanding loans; according to Bryan, Jenkins had to know that even if he did want to take his own life his family would be better off if he waited a matter of weeks. "If he did commit suicide, he showed damned poor timing," Bryan said recently. But the people who felt closest to Jenkins thought that he wouldn't commit suicide no matter how bad a spot he found himself in. "If that sheriff had been in a room for one minute with Johnny Jenkins, he'd know he's been barking up the wrong tree," Michael Parrish, the manager of the Jenkins Company, said not long after the sheriff's inclination to call Jenkins' death a suicide became public. "He'd know about the force of his personality, his confidence, his assurance to himself and to those around him that any problem could be overcome. What it gets down to is that the sheriff didn't know Johnny Jenkins."

And if Jenkins did shoot himself, his friends asked, why didn't his hand show evidence of gunpowder? And where was the gun? In fact, there were soon some theories about that circulating in Austin. The most popular was the plastic-Coke-bottle theory. If someone who wanted to make a suicide look like a murder attached the gun to a large plastic Coke bottle with holes in it, the theorists said, he would fall where he was shot but the gun would drift down the river until the bottle finally filled with water and sank. There was a kind of nutty offshoot of the Coke-bottle theory whose name describes it: the helium-balloon theory. Without endorsing either of those theories, Sheriff Keirsey said that finding the gun would not be essential to concluding that Jenkins had committed suicide. He has since said that the gun is probably still in the river, around where Jenkins' body was found. "Just because we haven't found it doesn't mean it isn't there," he said, pointing out that when he was on the homicide squad in Austin the police often failed to recover a gun from the Colorado River even after being told precisely where it had been thrown in.

The sheriff didn't put much stock in the fact that the test for Jenkins' having fired a gun came up negative. He has said that the results could have been caused by the body's having been in the river for a couple of hours, and forensic specialists agree that, even aside from the effects of the Colorado's current, a negative test is not proof that the person tested did not fire a gun. The sheriff was never impressed by either of the two most widespread notions of why Jenkins might have been murdered. A robber, Sheriff Keirsey has said, would probably have turned the wallet inside out and rifled the car and given more evidence of having been at the scene. The notion that Jenkins had been killed by Las Vegas mobsters over a gambling debt made no sense to the sheriff. "If you seem to be welshing on a gambling debt, the first thing they want to do is to put some hurt on you—break your legs, smash up your face, do some odds and ends," he has said. "If they do have to kill you, they'd make it obvious, to leave a message." From his investigations, the sheriff came to believe that John Jenkins was facing a financial crisis far beyond whatever money problems he had managed to deal with in the past. He also came to believe that Jenkins was facing the prospect of being expelled from the A.B.A.A. because of the forgery scandal and the prospect of being indicted for setting the 1987 fire. (The sheriff is mistaken about the A.B.A.A. expulsion. The chairman of the ethics committee had asked Jenkins, in a telephone conversation, to write him a letter giving some details about the provenance of some documents—the committee was particularly concerned about indications that one document might have been resold by the Jenkins Company after it was returned as inauthentic—but that was many steps away from any thought of expulsion. The state fire marshal's office will say only that the investigation of the 1987 fire was still going on and that Jenkins had not been eliminated as a suspect.) The insistence of Jenkins' friends that he was simply not the sort of person who would commit suicide did not persuade Sheriff Keirsey. He came to believe that Jenkins was just the sort of person who, if he decided to commit suicide, would make it appear to be murder. "He wouldn't be the typical suicide profile," the sheriff said recently, after pointing out the various problems that had piled up on Jenkins. "He was a superegotistical guy and a superintelligent guy. They're not going to go out here and tell you they give up. But his esteem and his prestige and his status had diminished in the last year or so, and he couldn't live with the stigma of defeat. His family says he was always able to pull out, but pretty soon you use your coupons up."

The county official whose responsibility it was to decide officially how John Jenkins met his death—a justice of the peace named B. T. Henderson—did not come to the same conclusion. Henderson also has a law-enforcement background, and he's proud of it. "I'm an old-time peace officer myself," he said recently. "My father was killed as a peace officer. My grandfather was a peace officer. When the sheriff was a cadet at the police academy in Austin, I was the chief of police of Ingleside, Texas, down near Corpus Christi." Explaining the decision he came to, Henderson said, "I went by the evidence at the scene and the autopsy. The sheriff was going on assumptions—halfhearted stories told to him by people who wouldn't swear to them and wouldn't testify to them in court. He was using a lot of what-ifs." When it was up to him to rule officially about what had happened at the boat ramp, Henderson said, "It's my official ruling that Mr. John Holmes Jenkins III came to his death at the hands of a person or persons unknown."

To some extent, whether people agree with the conclusions of the sheriff or those of the justice of the peace depends on what they thought of John Jenkins when he was alive. His friends tend to find it difficult to believe that a man whose brains and confidence and resourcefulness they so admired simply gave up. Some people who didn't like Jenkins find it easy to believe that a man whose profligate ways and shady practices finally caught up with him shot himself rather than face the music. Jenkins' friends say that the sheriff would rather assume that Jenkins committed suicide than look for a murderer. The sheriff says that Jenkins simply didn't live the sort of life his family would like to think he did. Since the first week or so after the body was discovered, there hasn't been any significant evidence to bolster the argument of either side. After the justice of the peace handed down his ruling, he said, "Whether the sheriff pursues it is his business," and Michael Parrish said recently of the sheriff, "Since he's not very interested in finding a murderer, he's not going to waste much time on it." Both in Austin and in Bastrop County, there's a feeling that there may never be much more known about what happened to John Jenkins at the boat ramp that Sunday.

Dorman David now lives quietly in Pass Christian, Mississippi, with his wife and a couple of kids, and makes sculpture. He says that he is finally off drugs and drink, and that he has pretty much run out of mud money. At fifty-one, he's a large, amiable man—a former amateur heavyweight boxer who has put on a few pounds since his fighting days. David, understandably, is not fond of the notion that he was John Jenkins' patsy. "There were no bad trades with Jenkins," he said not long ago. "He didn't win at trades with me, and he didn't win at poker with me." According to David, Jenkins was not even a spectacular poker player in those days. "He was up and coming, but he was always overplaying his hand," David said. "It was his ego problem, which is the only reason you lose at poker or anything else. The ego problem is all there is to deal with in life. First you have to be able to see it, and then you have to be able to deal with it." After David finally stumbled out of the book business, in the early seventies, he saw neither Jenkins nor William Simpson. Although Simpson is semi-retired these days, he can often be found at the same Houston auction gallery, which his son now runs. Not long ago, he told a visitor that the gallery doesn't use historical documents much these days to vary the menu of its auctions, having turned more toward the autographs of entertainers ("dead entertainers, not live entertainers—people who can't get their little fingers around a pencil"). He expressed great sadness about the death of John Jenkins. "The truth is," Simpson said, "that he was a very complex person, not a simple man."

The Jenkins estate has had difficulty collecting on one life-insurance policy, for reasons that are unconnected with the way Jenkins died, but the policies that lenders held on Jenkins' life have freed the company from the constant pressure of debt for the first time in its history. "Ironically, this has made them solvent," an old acquaintance of Jenkins' said recently. The plant—the building that was due to be auctioned off for debt on the steps of the Travis County Courthouse—is now owned outright by the Jenkins Company. The company seems to be more of a presence in the book business than it was in the last few years of John Jenkins' life. Since last April, it has put out three catalogues. Those who tend to tie the rise and fall of John Jenkins to the Texas economy point out that this is not a great time for a debt-ridden high roller to be operating in Texas. They say that, sad as it may be to contemplate, the Jenkins Company is better off with John Jenkins' insurance money than it would be with John Jenkins.

Bookdealers all over the world had their say about the death of John Jenkins. Some people talked of him as a bold and imaginative pioneer, and some as an egotistical and untrustworthy manipulator. There was even an obituary, by a bookman named Tobias Rodgers, in the *Independent,* one of London's most respected dailies. It was an obituary that probably would have pleased Jenkins—because it was essentially sympathetic and because it was in such a prominent English publication and because it put the price of the Eberstadt purchase at more than ten million dollars. "He was an erratically blazing light in a rather dim world, and above all a constantly kind, gentle man," Rodgers wrote. "He described him-

self in one of his writings as the 'Baron Munschausen of Books.'
Characteristically for one who thought so big and was so slapdash
in small things he spelt the name wrongly." There was a lot of talk
about how much Johnny Jenkins would have enjoyed the attention—talk that Michael Parrish, for one, resented. "People say,
'Oh, it's Johnny's last scam,'" Parrish said a couple of months after Jenkins' death. "They say, 'He pulled the wool over everyone's
eyes. He's up there laughing.' But it's hard to laugh when you're
dead. It's hard to reap the benefits of killing yourself." Still, people
do tend to imagine scenarios. Jerry Conn, the Austin writer who
knew Jenkins as a child in Beaumont, has imagined an ending to
the mystery which he believes would be pure Johnny Jenkins. "I
like to think that he developed a great story with a kicker," Conn
said. "He wrote a novel and a movie script and he sent it to someone in Kathmandu. And he said, 'In a year, send this to my wife and
the proceeds are to go to my estate, *and I'm to get proper credit.*' If
it doesn't have that part, it's not Jenkins. And people would read
the novel and see the movie, and they'd say, 'Oh, that guy! What a
character! What a great man!'"

—1989

IF THE BOOT FITS . . .

W hile George W. Bush was running for president in 2000, I wrote a poem entitled "A Scientific Observation on the Speaking Problems That Seem to Run in the Bush Family":

> He thinks that *hostile's hostage*.
> He cannot say *subliminal*.
> The way Bush treats the language
> Is bordering on criminal.
>
> His daddy had the problem.
> He used the nounless predicate.
> Those cowboy boots can do that
> To people from Connecticut.

If we subject this poem to close textual analysis—something, I must admit, that nobody has ever bothered to do with any of my poems before—we can see clearly that it makes two points. For one, the mangled syntax of George W. Bush, the forty-third president of the United States is shown to exist in at least two generations of the Bush family. Since no one questions the intelligence of George H. W. Bush—who was, after all, elected to Phi Beta Kappa—this amounts to a refutation of the theory that the younger Bush speaks the way he does because he's not smart enough to speak any other way. That theory has always had strong proponents, particularly after details of George W. Bush's academic record and his business career began to leak out, but, speaking personally, I am happy to be rid of it. I think it's dispiriting to discuss whether or not the president of the United States—what used to be called the leader of the Free World until the Patriot Act and Guantanamo Bay made that phrase sound sarcastic—is simply a doofus.

The second point is hinted at by the word "scientific" in the po-em's title. Rereading that title a few years after it was written, I re-alized that I had postulated what scientists call a hypothesis—the hypothesis that cramming the feet of high-born Eastern-seaboard preppies into cowboy boots can lead to speech difficulties. Far-fetched, you say? It isn't so far, in fact, from the hypothesis that forcing a naturally left-handed child to become right-handed can lead to stuttering or, for that matter, from the hypothesis I con-cocted some years ago to see if I could cause a brief panic on Wall Street—that wearing red suspenders instead of a belt can lower the sperm count.

Once I realized that my cowboy-boots breakthrough was a hypothesis, I was surprised that there had been no significant response from the scientific community. As I have always un-derstood the scientific method, once someone postulates a hy-pothesis, researchers test it through such devices as laboratory experiments, longitudinal studies, and—in this case, I would as-sume—extensive interviews with a significant sampling of boot salesmen in places like Lubbock and Wichita Falls ("Yes, sir, when he first came in here—walked in wearing some of them Docksid-ers, they call 'em, with no socks—he was talkin' away just as pretty as you please . . . .") I know that President George W. Bush himself has spoken out vigorously for thoroughness in scientific inves-tigation—global warming and evolution are just two of the areas where he has indicated that there is considerable work left to be done before the verdict is in—and yet there has been no sustained effort to test my hypothesis.

I had assumed that, at the very least, some of those hotshot Washington reporters would use my poem as a takeoff point for the sort of probing questions they like to trot out for televised press conferences. Is it true, for instance, that those members of the Bush clan who remained in what the geopolitical types might call "the Greenwich Country Day sphere of influence" express themselves with great fluidity, except for those who keep their teeth tightly clenched in the high-WASP delivery sometimes referred to as Locust Valley lockjaw? Or is a breakdown in sentence structure a widespread Old Money affectation, like frayed button-downs and peeling paint? Could it be that one of the secret rituals of Skull and Bones is foot binding? If cowboy boots have no effect on behavior or syntax, why do western ranch hands refer to a visitor from the East as a tenderfoot? Where does the penny loafer stand in all of this?

When it comes to the answers to these questions, I am willing to let the chips fall where they may. I'm aware that some people will say that I am making too much of the effect cowboy boots could have on what I think could be fairly described as effete feet. They will argue that although a drastic change of footwear could conceivably affect pronunciation and fluidity, it could never cause the sort of thought process that brings George W. Bush to utter a sentence like "Free societies will be allies against these hateful few who have no conscience, who kill at the whim of a hat," or "Our enemies will never stop searching for new ways to harm our country, and neither will I."

But footwear is symbolic of a much broader cultural dislocation suffered by the Bush family. These are people who switched rather suddenly from finger sandwiches to fried pork rinds, and then switched back again every summer when they returned to Kennebunkport. These are people who grew up listening to pleasant Episcopalian vicars sermonize on the need to be kind to one's servants and now find themselves locked in a partnership with preachers like Jerry Falwell, who believes that God calls up hurricanes to smite those who demonstrate a tolerance of The Homosexual Lifestyle.

Could it be that if the Bush family had been given the luxury of making these and other cultural changes more gradually, both of the Bush presidents would be speaking in perfectly parsed paragraphs? I offer as evidence for the affirmative William Jefferson Clinton, of Hot Springs, Arkansas. Clinton must have known what could happen to the rhetorical skills of someone who, as they say in the South, "strayed too far from his raisin'." Despite his gold-chip education, he clung to the culture of Arkansas so tightly that his Secret Service code name was Bubba and it was easy to imagine him in the Oval Office at about nine-thirty in the morning swigging a ten-ounce bottle of Coke with goobers in it. Yes, of course, the man had his faults as president. But he spoke like an angel.

—2005

NEW CHEERLEADERS

For a number of years, there was a place for a Mexican-American among the four cheerleaders of Crystal City High School, more or less the way there was a Jewish seat on the Supreme Court. It was nothing official, but townspeople who went out to the football game to cheer on the Hawgs (known officially as the Javelins, the name given the wild boars found in South Texas) could be confident that three out of the four girls leading them in cheers would be non-Mexican-American whites—the people known in the Southwest as Anglos. Only about fifteen per cent of the people in Crystal City are Anglos, but they had always been accustomed to leading the high-school cheers or anything else that was considered at all important to lead. A lot of the Mexican-Americans in Crystal City migrate to the Midwest for farm work from spring to fall and support themselves off and on in Crystal City during the winter by picking spinach or onions or working in the Del Monte plant. When the schools were segregated in Crystal City, only an elementary school had to be provided for Mexican-Americans, since virtually all of them dropped out before high school anyway.

Even in the late forties, a Crystal City High School graduating class consisted typically of twenty-five or thirty Anglos and one or two Mexican-Americans. Gradually, the percentage of Mexican-Americans in the high school grew, until it nearly reflected the Mexican-American majority in the town. But the student organizations and activities remained basically Anglo—partly because the Anglos had the self-confidence that comes from having always run things, partly because a lot of Mexican-American students didn't take much interest, partly because the overwhelmingly Anglo faculty and administration arranged it that way. The football team, which was ordinarily dominated by Anglos, elected its own Football Sweetheart, but the baseball team, which always had a Mexican-American majority, was told to elect two Baseball Sweethearts—one Mexican-American and one Anglo. Honors such as Most Beautiful or Most Representative were distributed by methods that included faculty committees and even sending pictures off to someone like Troy Donahue or Glen Campbell for judging—but rarely included popular elections. And the teachers selecting cheerleaders always seemed to settle on one Mexican-American and three Anglos. In Crystal City, having Anglo cheerleaders was one symbol to the Anglos that their high school was still effectively Anglo even after becoming predominantly Mexican-American. It happened to be the same kind of symbol to the Mexican-American students: after the usual cheerleader selection was made in the spring of 1969, they began a protest that eventually led to Crystal City's having all Mexican-American cheerleaders, a Mexican-American majority on the school board, a Mexican-American superintendent, a lot of Mexican-American teachers, and a lot of enraged Anglos.

In quieter times, Crystal City was best known for calling itself the Spinach Capital of the World—or, really, for symbolizing that claim with a statue of Popeye in front of the municipal building. It's a town of nine thousand, about a hundred miles southwest of San Antonio, in a part of South Texas called the Winter Garden—dry scrubland developed fifty or sixty years ago when it was discovered that a winter crop of vegetables could be produced on it. Although Crystal City has always had a certain number of open, straightforward bigots, it has not been the kind of place in which Anglo control is maintained by violence or even by denying Mexican-Americans the right to vote. The Anglos own everything. They like to tell visitors about the decent, hard-working Mexicans they grew up with—Mexicans who would have been appalled at people who wanted something for nothing or at people who tried to create friction between the races. Having taken political as well as economic control more or less for granted, the Anglos were startled in 1963 when, after a quiet registration campaign conducted by the Teamsters and some other outside organizers, the

Mexican-Americans took over the city council—a victory that is sometimes spoken of as the beginning of political activism among Mexican-Americans in Texas. But those elected had little experience, no local organization that extended much past the election victory in ideology or commitment, and no continuing help from those who organized the campaign—one theory being that Texas liberals were so accustomed to participating in glorious defeats that an actual victory left them too stunned to continue. The Anglos were soon back in control.

At first, the student protest in 1969 seemed manageable. The school superintendent decided that the Mexican-Americans as well as the Anglos would have three cheerleaders, and the school year ended with the Hawg teams' being bi-ethnically cheered toward victory. But the following fall the protest was still alive. The alumni association had announced plans to choose a Homecoming Queen, to be elected by the alumni from among high-school girls who had at least one parent who had graduated from Crystal City High School—an eligibility requirement that meant almost no Mexican-American girls even qualified for rejection. The Mexican-American students—who increasingly tended to refer to themselves as Chicanos rather than Mexican-Americans—began arguing not only about the Homecoming Queen but about the need for bilingual education and about the inequities of tests based on cultural background and about discrimination or neglect by Anglo teachers. In December, they began to boycott the school.

It is traditional to blame outside agitators for such protests, and the Anglos of Crystal City blamed a young man named José Ángel Gutiérrez, who did in fact have all the attributes of an outside agitator except that he was born in Crystal City and had been the president of the 1962 senior class at Crystal City High School. The son of a doctor, Gutiérrez had been the kind of student Anglos liked to point to as an example of how a bright and ambitious Mexican-American could get ahead. After high school, Gutiérrez went off to San Antonio to win a master's degree in government. But then, after founding a militant Chicano group called the Mexican-American Youth Organization, he came back to Crystal

City as an organizer—with the announced intention of engineering a Mexican-American takeover in three Winter Garden counties. As an organizing tool for Gutiérrez, the boycott became a movement—with mass meetings in the plaza of the neighborhood known as Mexico Chico and shouts of "Viva La Raza!" and reluctant adults' being drawn in by the participation of their children. After a month, the school board granted most of the student demands. The boycott organization remained intact, and that spring Gutiérrez and two other Chicanos ran for the school board as candidates of La Raza Unida, a third party for Texas Chicanos that Gutiérrez had helped found. The Raza school-board candidates won (as did those who were trying to capture the city council), and joined with a Mexican-American already on the board to form a four-to-three majority. The majority's first act was to elect José Ángel Gutiérrez president of the Crystal City school board—not quite the sort of getting ahead the Anglos had in mind. The school-board meetings, formerly held in a conference room, had to be moved to the high-school cafeteria and then to the high-school auditorium in order to accommodate the citizens who wanted to ask questions or state opinions or shout "Viva!"

The Anglos in town are often at a loss for words hideous enough to describe Gutiérrez, although they ordinarily make do with "Communist" until one comes to mind. His past as the model honor student of Crystal City High School has meant not that he is considered less of an outside agitator but merely that he is considered an outside agitator who also happens to be an ingrate. Conversations with Crystal City Anglos about Gutiérrez almost always include stories of how some of his dedicated Anglo teachers used to drive him to far-off public-speaking and debating engagements when he was in high school. "In their own cars," the speaker will often say, shaking his head at how far ingratitude can go. "With their own gas."

In return, Anglos say, Gutiérrez has come back to Crystal City to divide the races rather than bring them together—an accusation Gutiérrez doesn't really deny, since he operated from the start on the theory that the only way to build a movement to give Mexican-Americans some political power in Crystal City would be to shake them from their dependence on Anglos and Anglo values. Gutiérrez still provides some gringo-baiting speeches for the local Anglos to point to in horror, and no human-relations specialist will ever use the first year of Mexican-American control of the Crystal City schools as an example of how to make a transition as painless as possible for the people who were used to being in control. The new board not only began bilingual education and established the federal free-lunch program in the high school but also declared Mexican Independence Day a half-day school holiday and banned nonunion lettuce from the cafeterias. Anglo teachers who were considered insensitive to their Mexican-American students have not had their contracts renewed. An Anglo who had been hired as superintendent just before the election and given a three-year contract ("to preserve continuity," one of the Anglo board members has said) was fired despite his contract, accused of not implementing the board's new policies. The armed-services recruiters who had always made routine stops at Crystal City High School were informed that they would no longer be permitted on school property. (In the board's reasoning, the traditional assumption that the relatively few Mexican-American boys who did make it through high school would go right into the service had prevented some of them from considering the possibility of college and had been partly responsible for the fact that eleven of them had been killed in Vietnam. The realities of military conscription were not ignored; the board appointed a draft counsellor to advise students—and teachers—of their rights.) The school board passed a resolution opposing the war in Vietnam. The school board accepted the transfer of boycotting Chicano students from another South Texas town. The school board banned intelligence testing. For a while, the school board even placed a moratorium on corporal punishment—a break with Crystal City tradition that proved too radical even for José Ángel Gutiérrez, who eventually settled for a set of safeguards to protect the rights of the students being paddled.

Of all the changes made, nothing has angered the Anglos more than the new practice of the band director's announcing half-time formations at the high-school football game in Spanish as well as English. The same Anglo students who say they have nothing at all against the start being made in bilingual education find it difficult to talk about the band director's Spanish without raising their voices and repeating "This is the United States of America" again and again. The first time the director spoke Spanish over the press-box public-address system at the Crystal City football field, someone turned out the press-box lights. Throughout the season, the reaction to the Spanish was so raucous—with shouts of "Go back to Mexico!" from the Anglos and "Viva La Raza!" from the Chicanos—that the band director began walking up through the stands to the press box in the company of two Chicano bodyguards. The Chicanos say that Spanish translations are not unreasonable in a town where many of the students' parents and grandparents have an uncertain grasp of English. But the Anglos believe that the director—a Raza Unida supporter—started speaking Spanish only to provoke them. The Anglo students were particularly upset when the Spanish translations were used even for away games. There, for all the people in Carrizo Springs or Uvalde to see, would be Crystal City High School with Mexican-American cheerleaders and a band that played the Mexican "Jalisco" as well as the old Hawg fight song and a half-time show being announced in Spanish—a Chicano school.

The Anglos retaliated with constant letters in the county weekly—most of them signed by an anonymous citizens' committee—accusing the board of crimes ranging from political firings to sloppiness in handling the cafeteria funds. The citizens' committee sent a letter around asking Anglos to withhold their school taxes, and some of them did—including one of the Anglo members of the school board, a local rancher. (At the last meeting before the rancher's term expired, Gutiérrez, to the delight of the large crowd of Mexican-Americans in attendance, refused to count the rancher's vote because of the tax delinquency. When the rancher read a statement suggesting that "there is being propagated in our own school a system of ideas that is alien to our American way of life," a woman in the audience shouted, "Go ahead and pay your taxes, and then you talk!")

A lot of Anglos who didn't withhold taxes or write letters to the county weekly were confident that the school board would be recaptured, just as the city council had been recaptured. "Your Mexican'll always revert," a local rancher said recently. Two seats on the board came up this month, and, in the belief that people with Anglo names no longer win elections in Crystal City, the Anglos ran two candidates who are actually Mexican-Americans—people thought of by La Raza Unida supporters as *vendidos*, or sellouts. They were easily defeated by La Raza Unida candidates. The victory means that La Raza Unida is guaranteed control of the board for several years, no matter how many times Mexicans revert, and next fall Anglos will have to face the decision of whether to pull their children out of school or move from Crystal City or make some accommodation.

At Crystal City High School, Anglos and Chicanos lead separate lives. The Anglos say the division is a result of Gutiérrez' racism; the Chicanos say it's merely that the division that always existed is now acknowledged by both sides. Some people say that the classes are slightly less orderly, and some people say that Chicanos are now slightly more willing to speak up. The Anglos who played in the band have quit, and so have the Anglos who were on the staff of the yearbook. They give a variety of reasons. Chicanos say that what is really bothering the Anglo students is the same thing that is bothering their parents—that they are no longer in charge. There are some Anglo students who talk openly about their belief that Mexican-Americans are constitutionally incapable of being in charge. A conversation about changes in the school can sometimes lead to talk about Mexican-Americans' returning from the Midwest with new cars to drive to the welfare office. A few of the Anglo students acknowledge that there might have been some inequities in the past. But the most widespread attitude among them seems to be a feeling of having been personally injured by the injection of racism and politics and hatred into a school that they and their families had found so friendly and comfortable for so many years. Like their parents, they always regarded the status quo as nonpolitical and the traditional arrangement of control by race as nonracist. "These are supposed to be a person's best years," a former cheerleader said recently. "And mine have been ruined."

—1971

WHOSE MINES ARE THEY?

"MORE MINES FOUND IN PERSIAN GULF
SHIPPING LANE"
—*New York Times*, July 29, 1987

I happened to meet Patrick O'Brien, the director of the Dallas Public Library, last week, and I immediately accused him of being behind the mining of the Persian Gulf. He denied it, but, then, he would, wouldn't he?

If I hadn't had overwhelming circumstantial evidence, I wouldn't have said anything. But there were too many facts that couldn't be explained away by a quick tongue and an easy command of the Dewey Decimal System.

The oil-glut recession that started in places like Houston and Wichita Falls spread long ago to the entire state of Texas, and the budget of the Dallas Public Library has suffered accordingly. In Texas these days, about the only cheerful economic news is whatever news there is about threats to the Middle East oil supply. Every time an oil tanker in the Persian Gulf gets spooked by a mine, the price of a barrel of West Texas crude goes up a penny or two and the financial prospects for the Dallas Public Library's book purchasing fund look a little brighter. Need you know more?

I've been on to this sort of thing for years. Once you realize that international events have a serious effect on local American economies, you don't have to be Sherlock Holmes to catch these jokers. Ten or 15 years ago, the city of New York, which had been on the brink of bankruptcy, was starting to prosper mightily partly because real estate prices had been pushed up by foreigners who were desperate to get their money out of countries that seemed vulnerable to radicals and terrorists. I realized that the New York real estate sharks who had once been so generous with the United Way and the Jewish Federation and the Federation of Catholic

Charities must have all switched their charitable contributions to the Communist Party of Milan. They denied it, but, then, they would, wouldn't they?

At the beginning of the oil glut, in fact, there was a lot of talk in Texas about how the whole thing could be put right if some Texas oil tycoon just flew a bunch of commandos deep into one of those Arab deserts so they could take out a couple of miles of pipeline. When that didn't happen, some people figured it was probably because the talk hadn't really been serious. That's not what I figured. I figured that the commandos had been laid on but that any Texas tycoon who might have been willing to fly them in had by then had his Lear jet repossessed.

But laying mines would be a lot easier. You could do it in a bass boat. And I'd bet that instructions on how to do it could be found right there in the library. I've personally heard O'Brien say in public that the library had information on virtually every subject imaginable.

So I asked O'Brien where he was on the night all those mines were laid in the Persian Gulf a couple of weeks ago. He said he didn't remember, although he assumed he was out somewhere begging money.

Well, what more evidence do you need than that? He had the motive. He had the wherewithal. O'Brien, remember, is a professional librarian. If he looks up mines, he's not going to find himself reading about King Solomon's Mines or the zinc mining industry in southwestern Missouri.

I know there are people who are saying that O'Brien couldn't have laid all those mines on his own. Of course he couldn't have. But he could have easily found confederates. The people connected with any number of impoverished Texas cultural institutions would be well suited to commando raids. The undercover work would be done by actors from the regional theaters. Data on tides and water conditions would be provided by oceanographers from the University of Texas. Fake mines, good enough to start a little movement in the market for crude, could be fashioned by the art museums out of papier-mache and dropped off the bass boats by members of the ballet companies, moving gracefully to the music of "Swan Lake" on the bass boat's tape-deck.

The American public, of course, continues to assume that the mining is being done by the sort of Iranian patriots who were inspired to march right down to their nearest recruiting sergeant last summer when they heard that the Revolutionary Guard's Persian Gulf maneuvers were being called Operation Martyrdom. Nobody suspects O'Brien. Except me. I don't intend to turn him in—I have a selfish interest in large book-purchasing budgets myself—but I wanted him to know that I knew. Before we parted, I whispered to him what I figure is the true code name for what's happening in the Gulf: Operation Major Funding. He denied it, but, he would, wouldn't he?

—1987

NOT SUPER-OUTRAGEOUS

In August of 1968, Lee Otis Johnson, the noisiest black militant in Houston, was convicted of giving away one marijuana cigarette and was sentenced to thirty years in the penitentiary. There are people in Houston who believe Johnson was treated unjustly, but nobody of any prominence has ever said so publicly. Even among people who are doing whatever they can to get Johnson out of prison, a sense of outrage about the case is considered a bit naïve. "We make a big thing of it," one of them said recently. "But in Texas it's not really so super-outrageous." In Texas, a jury or judge can give a defendant ninety-nine years for sale or possession of marijuana, and some of them have. Any marijuana sentence sounds mild compared to the sentences handed out for violent crime lately in Dallas, where some juries, in an effort to counter a parole system considered ruinously enlightened, have sent people to jail for several hundred years for rape or a thousand for armed robbery. Last summer, a man convicted in Dallas of selling three caps of heroin was sentenced to fifteen hundred years in the penitentiary. It is said that one Fort Worth man who was given five hundred years or so stopped on his way out of the courtroom and said to the judge, "Judge, I'm not sure I can serve that sentence."

"Well, you do the best you can," the judge replied.

The backers of Lee Otis Johnson maintain that, unlike someone caught with a hundred pounds of marijuana or convicted of armed robbery, Johnson was punished for activities that had nothing to do with the charge in court. But not many people in Houston would find that outrageous or even surprising. When the Houston district attorney, Carol Vance, is asked why he chose to try Johnson's one-marijuana-cigarette case personally, after having left virtually all other cases to his fifty or so assistants, he replies that Johnson was a dangerous man. "Everyone's got a right to criticize," the District Attorney has explained. "But when you start trying to encourage people to burn the city, that's a different matter." Johnson was never arrested for inciting to riot or for conspiracy to commit arson, but it is now customary in many parts of the country to use the marijuana laws for imprisoning people considered dangerous by district attorneys whether whatever makes them dangerous is against the law or not. John Sinclair, the leader of an organization called the White Panthers, was convicted in Detroit of possession of two marijuana cigarettes and is now serving a prison sentence of nine and a half to ten years. The *Texas Observer*, a durable liberal biweekly published in Austin, recently carried an account by Dave Beckwith of the trial of four black students from the University of California at Santa Barbara who were charged with possession of marijuana while travelling through Dallas and were presented to the town as captured black militants. Not long after sentencing two of them to three years in the penitentiary, the judge was quoted by the Dallas *News* as saying, "We had pretty good reason to believe that they were members of the Black Panther organization, dedicated to the overthrow of the government by revolution, but we couldn't prove that."

The *Observer* piece pointed out that the judge's own son had been arrested on a marijuana charge and given two years' probation, which is the customary penalty for nonpolitical whites who fail to have the charges dropped or the case indefinitely continued—the alternative sentence being a minimum of two years in prison for possession and five years for selling. (A Houston lawyer who specializes in such cases has handled thirty or forty of them successfully without yet having had to face a jury, and has come to believe that one reason the law making marijuana a felony is not changed is that "for lawyers it is the single most lucrative crime.") In Texas, except in cases in which the defendant is thought to be an important pusher, someone who is sent to jail for possession or sale of a small amount of marijuana is likely to be black or Mexican-American, and someone who is sent to jail for a long time is likely to be the kind of man district attorneys consider dangerous, and someone who is sent to jail for thirty years is, it follows as a matter of course, the noisiest black militant in Houston. When Texans interested in such matters hear about a long sentence for marijuana, their natural question is not how much marijuana the defendant had but who he is. "He was Mexican and political and in the Panhandle," a man active in the Houston American Civil Liberties Union said recently about one such defendant. "And that's a bad combination."

The A.C.L.U. man did not sound outraged. In Houston, it has been routine to use all sorts of laws in any way they can serve to maintain the climate of order—a climate that is considered necessary to the hyper-modern, hyper-expanding kind of prosperity the city prides itself on. In Houston, a professor and his teen-age daughter were arrested for passing out anti-war handbills, a Rice student who engaged in some guerrilla theatre during an anti-war demonstration was sentenced to six months for wearing the distinctive parts of an Army uniform, and a group of Mexican-Americans who knocked over some furniture during a demonstration at the school board this fall were indicted not only for disorderly conduct but also for "felony malicious mischief," which carries a penalty of up to twenty years. After a federal court ordered Houston's mayor and city council to grant a parade permit to a peaceful anti-war group, they passed an ordinance requiring an insurance fee from any group that wanted to parade in the future, and then openly discussed ways of getting around the law so that the American Legion, which claimed poverty, could have its parade anyway. There are a lot of people who would consider using the law in this way a threat to civil liberties, but not many of them live in Houston. The District Attorney asked only that Lee Otis Johnson be sent to jail for twenty years; it was a jury of twelve white citizens that decided on thirty. The Houston police chief has expressed views on civil liberties considerably less sympathetic than those of the District Attorney—whose definition of dangerous men does distinguish between "revolutionaries" and people who are "just raising hell"—and the chief seems to have been given an award by just about every organization in Houston that has the resources to hold a luncheon and have a plaque made up. When the chief was given the Sons of the American Revolution good-citizenship award this fall, the Houston *Chronicle* account of his acceptance speech began, "Police Chief Herman Short has chastized a society that will allow an organization such as the American Civil Liberties Union to fight prayer in the school on one hand and defend dissenters and revolutionaries on the other."

In this atmosphere, Houston, now the sixth-largest city in the country, still has the kind of endemic right-wing violence that used to be associated with small, mean towns in the more backward areas of Alabama. Night riders who fire shotgun blasts at the home of an anti-war leader or the office of an underground paper are routine. The Family Hand, a restaurant that caters to Houston's long-hair community, has been fire-bombed twice. A local television newscaster may be threatened for showing pictures of the My Lai massacre, and a local theatre may be stink-bombed for showing "Guess Who's Coming to Dinner?" The listener-sponsored radio station that the Pacifica Foundation opened in Houston in March—a station that regularly aired the kind of news and opinions that Houston citizens can count on their newspapers to avoid mentioning—had its transmitter blown up in May, got back on the air in June, and was bombed off again in October. (The station's manager, Larry Lee, who has attempted to keep some rough record of terrorist incidents in Houston, was recently accused by a man from the *Chronicle* of becoming paranoid. "You may be right," Lee said. "I keep imagining somebody is blowing up my transmitter.") The Ku Klux Klan is often mentioned as being behind the night-riding, but nobody has ever been charged, and the most noted comment of the police chief about the Klan was less than threatening. "I am not a Klansman and I know of no police officer who is a Klansman," he said after the Grand Dragon had announced that a lot of police officers were in the Klan—a statement unlikely to be challenged by anyone in the black community. "You can't fault a man, however, for praising God, country, and obedience to law and order. That's what we all stand for." Black people in Houston assume that Lee Otis Johnson was jailed for his political activities; a lot of them assume that he was framed. But, then, a lot of them assume that Carl Hampton, who succeeded Johnson as the noisiest black militant in Houston and died in a gun battle, was murdered by the police. So, in a way, thirty years in jail for giving away a marijuana cigarette is not really super-outrageous.

"You've got to remember that in most people's minds Lee Otis Johnson was a loudmouthed nigger who called a lot of names and seemed to go out of his way to irritate everybody," a local man who has followed the Johnson case said recently. Many white people in Houston thought that thirty years was just what a man like Lee Otis Johnson deserved; many other white people thought that thirty years was what a man like Lee Otis Johnson might have expected from twelve white people in Houston. In terms of accepting the decision as non-outrageous, the two views amounted to the same thing. After the conviction, an organization of social workers expressed doubt whether Johnson could have received a fair trial in Houston, and a grand jury, in calling for reform of the marijuana laws, contrasted the thirty-year sentence (without mentioning Johnson's name) with a sentence of two years' probation that had been given a convicted murderer at about the same time. That seems to have been the extent of public outcry. Not many white people in Houston wanted to be involved in any way with Lee Otis Johnson. A kind of free-lance militant who had first come to attention as a S.N.C.C. leader at Texas Southern University, he provided headlines like "LOCAL SNCC LOOKS TO REVOLUTION." (Although when an opportunity for widespread violence came, on the night that Martin Luther King died, he helped maintain calm in the city.) Black leaders tend to agree that Johnson presented some danger to the white people who run Houston—not because he was likely to organize a revolution but because he had a peculiar ability to communicate with ordinary black people and a peculiar ability to infuriate white people like the mayor and the chief of police.

By the standards of the Houston Police Department, Johnson certainly qualified as a dangerous man: at about the time of his trial, a member of the department's intelligence unit who specialized in spying on civil-rights and anti-war groups told David Brand, of the

Wall Street Journal, that the tipoff on Communist influence was when someone "talks about social change." The Houston police picked up Johnson so often that it became a kind of routine. The drug charge almost seemed another in a series of arrests that normally resulted in his being fined or in the charges' being dropped. It came six weeks after Johnson had allegedly given a marijuana cigarette to a police undercover man (the delay, the police later said, was necessary to protect the agent), and some of Johnson's supporters spoke of it as an obvious manifestation of the mayor's pique, since it came only a couple of days after a memorial rally for King at which Johnson had been wildly cheered and the mayor had been booed. The trial was short. Johnson's lawyer asked for a continuance until the mayor and the police chief were available to testify; it was his contention that they had conspired to harass and eventually entrap Johnson in order to prevent "his further exercise of his rights of free speech and assembly." When the motion was denied, he presented no other witnesses. The prosecution called the undercover man and a couple of policemen who testified that the cigarette had been given to them to check and was indeed marijuana. Within a few hours, Johnson was in jail, starting his thirty years, and he has been in jail ever since.

Johnson's appeal has now been through the state courts, and it will soon be taken to federal district court. Among lawyers who have read the transcript, there is agreement that it contains nothing legally outrageous. The hope of some Johnson supporters is that some court—if not the district court or the court of appeals, then the Supreme Court—will decide that it is wrong to sentence a "dangerous man" to thirty years for giving away one marijuana cigarette and will then use something like the judge's refusal to grant a change of venue as a way to order a new trial. Johnson's name is still brought up occasionally—when someone is given a probated sentence for murder or when there is a discussion of the marijuana laws or when people talk about the death of Carl Hampton. There is a Lee Otis Johnson Defense Committee in Houston. A petition was gathered for an appeal to the parole board, and during the recent election campaign a group of University of Houston students stopped a speech by the governor, Preston Smith, with shouts of "Free Lee Otis!" (The Governor, seizing a rare opportunity to ridicule two minority groups with one statement, told a group of businessmen that he thought the students were shouting "*frijoles*," just like 'beans' in South Texas.") Some advertisements and stories have appeared in Eastern papers and in the underground press, but these days any group that wants to focus attention on someone it considers a political prisoner has a lot of competition.

People in Houston who have followed the case still talk occasionally of why the jurors gave Johnson ten years more than the District Attorney asked for. The summer after King's death was, of course, a fearful time in American cities, and, according to the theory of one Houston lawyer, "they were probably just more scared of him than the D.A. was." The District Attorney believes that the jury may have been affected by the presence in court of several Johnson followers dressed in dashikis and African robes; among costumes commonly worn in Houston to symbolize reverence for a cultural heritage, the dashiki is looked upon as considerably more threatening than the cowboy outfit. There is also a theory—considered rather abstruse in Houston—that the jury may have actually been alarmed at the exchange of a marijuana cigarette as well as being alarmed at Johnson; marijuana was less common among white teen-agers in Houston two years ago than it is today, and more people still considered it the most dangerous weapon in Satan's arsenal. "If a girl wants to have a career as a syphilitic prostitute or if a boy wants to end in the electric chair because he has killed a grocer in a hijacking, there is no more practical beginning than this cigarette contained in this envelope," the prosecution said before the sentencing. "Any amount of marijuana, any amount of dope, is a shame and disgrace to this community, and its use and effects would be so evil that should I speak to you for a hundred years I couldn't describe it properly." District Attorney Vance says that he was surprised to hear a harsher sentence than he had asked for, but he has also said that Johnson may have been given less than he deserved. Before the sentencing, Vance introduced into the record a previous conviction for auto theft, and the head of the police intelligence unit—a man who was later quoted in the *Wall Street Journal* piece as calling black demonstrators "arrogant bastards looking for an issue"—testified that he had found Johnson to be a man of bad character. In a documentary that the Pacifica station put on between bombings, Vance was asked about the sentence and replied, "Here was a person who was furnishing marijuana, he was a troublemaker, he tried to stir up a riot, he was a person who'd been to the penitentiary twice before. And yet, even though he could have gotten ninety-nine years or life imprisonment—and the minimum being five years—he ended up with a thirty-year sentence. I don't see that this is a very unusual verdict."

—1970

THREE TEXANS IN SIX LINES

A SHORT HISTORY OF LLOYD BENTSEN'S
DEALINGS WITH SPECIAL INTERESTS

The man is known for quo pro quidness.
In Texas, that's how folks do bidness.

—1993

ON THE APPOINTMENT OF ALBERTO GONZALES
AS ATTORNEY GENERAL

The AG's to be one Alberto Gonzales—
Dependable, actually loyal *über alles*.

—2005

THE EFFECT ON HIS CAMPAIGN OF THE RELEASE OF
GEORGE W. BUSH'S COLLEGE TRANSCRIPT

Obliviously on he sails,
With marks not quite as good as Quayle's.

—1999

MAKING ADJUSTMENTS

"All the other lawyers in Houston are asleep."
Just before seven on a rainy Wednesday morning, I reminded the lawyers standing in line outside the Houston
District Office of the United States Immigration and Naturalization Service that their colleagues—corporation lawyers, tax lawyers, trust lawyers, even criminal lawyers—were still in bed. The
lawyers in line just nodded and pulled closer to the wall of the
building, attempting to draw some shelter from a short overhang.
The thought had apparently occurred to them before.

There were half a dozen lawyers in line, some of them accompanied by clients. Pressed against the building on the other side
of the entrance—an entrance set into an alcove that is protected
by a heavy iron gate—sixty or seventy people stood in a separate
line for the general public. A mobile snack bar had pulled up to the
curb across the street from the longer line, and the proprietor was
doing a fair business in hot coffee and doughnuts. The district office of the I.N.S.—what immigration lawyers in Houston refer to
simply as Immigration—occupies a two-story corner building a
mile or so south of the imposing forest of modern glass towers that
is now Houston's downtown. In the days of the city's phenomenal
growth, developers took giant strides around Houston, snatching up huge tracts of land for a shopping area here and an office
complex there; the neighborhood around Immigration looks like
one of the places they must have stepped over on their way to the
southwestern suburbs. There are still some private houses, a few
of them in need of a paint job, and some empty lots. The local office
of the state employment commission is around the corner, with
its own line. Next to where the snack truck had pulled up, there is a
wholesale fish company—an enterprise that was pointed out to me
when I said to the lawyers that standing in line must be less unpleasant in the summer. On the next corner from where the law-

yers line up, there is a Chinese noodle factory. Ed Prud'homme, a lawyer whose office is only a block from Immigration, occasionally manages to get invited to lunch at the factory; he has handled some immigration matters for the noodle people. The location of Prud'homme's office is a strong part of his identification among his colleagues of the immigration bar. When I was introduced to Prud'homme—a short, storytelling man with a gray beard and an Arkansas accent—he said, "My claim to fame is being the first one in this line." On the Wednesday in question, he was second.

Beaumont Martin had beaten him to Immigration. When Martin arrived, he reached into his attaché case, withdrew a contraption made of aluminum and canvas, unfolded it into a short stool, and sat down. Martin, who is six feet five, looked rather odd perched on the tiny stool, but he is a man who has always been more interested in being practical than in keeping up appearances. Early in his career, he decided that having a secretary did not make economic sense for him, so he gets by with an answering machine and his own typing. He takes only cases that do not disrupt the system he has worked out for processing applications effectively in the least amount of time—straightforward matters of an immigrant's obtaining permanent-resident status through being related to another permanent resident or through marrying a citizen or through being employed in a job that the Department of Labor certifies to be a job not sought after by any citizens with equivalent qualifications. Because he finds jumpsuits the most comfortable apparel, he wears nothing but jumpsuits—short-sleeved jumpsuits that he orders by mail from California. Not long ago, a testimonial dinner was held for Sam Williamson, the dean of the immigration bar in Houston, and Martin was moved by the importance of the occasion to vary his costume to the extent of wearing a specially designed black-tie jumpsuit. It did not turn out to be a gesture that caused him to blend in with the crowd, since the dinner was not black-tie.

Martin was instrumental in negotiating what immigration lawyers in Houston always refer to as the Agreement of May 17, 1982—an agreement that gave immigration lawyers their own line, on one side of the entrance. Before that, they had to stand in line with the general public, across from the fish wholesaler. That line is let inside the gate in gulps of twenty or so; on mornings when it happened to have a couple of hundred people in it, a lawyer who hadn't arrived before dawn could spend most of his day outside the building. Before May 17, 1982, a lot of lawyers got to know one another well standing in line in the pre-dawn hours outside Immigration. Beaumont Martin spent so many hours with Sam Williamson that they sometimes speak of each other as father and son—although Williamson is as small and contentious as Martin is tall and detached. Williamson was not one of the negotiators of the May 17th agreement. He has always regarded Immigration as the enemy. In the days when lawyers had to stand in the general line, it was apparently common for Williamson to respond to tardiness in opening the doors at seven-thirty by rattling the gate and inveighing against the insensitivity and mindlessness of bureaucrats. Williamson is the sort of elder statesman whose advice to his younger colleagues is usually something like "Don't let those bastards get you!"

Under the agreement of May 17, 1982, a lawyer can use the special lawyers' line and file papers with a special clerk on one predetermined day of the week, according to the first letter of his last name. Wednesday is for people whose names begin with letters "H" through "P." On Wednesdays, Frank Halim, who studied law in Bombay as well as in New York, is almost always at Immigration. So is Patrick Murphy, a former English professor, who handles immigration matters for Fulbright & Jaworski, one of Houston's huge downtown firms. His business usually concerns the non-immigrant visas available for intracompany transfers—what I heard referred to at times as fat-cat visas. The Wednesday crowd also includes Richard Prinz, one of the few immigration lawyers in Houston who regularly go to court—defending someone accused of smuggling aliens into the country, for instance, or someone the I.N.S. is trying to deport under a provision of the law that permits the deportation of permanent residents who have been convicted of a serious crime. Sam Williamson occasionally shows up on Wednesdays, too. His last name begins with "W," of course, but Williamson hates rules.

A lawyer who has come to Immigration to accompany a client at an interview has another wait ahead of him inside the building, but that wait may be enlivened by the opportunity to buttonhole a passing immigration examiner and press for information on some other case. An immigration lawyer often has a case that he is particularly eager to have moved along quickly. An immigration lawyer always has a case that has been maddeningly, inexplicably delayed. The Houston office is thought of as more efficient than most I.N.S. district offices, but, considering the reputation of most I.N.S. district offices, that is not the sort of compliment that someone might be tempted to frame and hang on the wall. When people who deal regularly with the I.N.S. try to illustrate the depths of its inefficiency and obduracy, they often find themselves at a loss for American institutions to compare it with, and turn to foreign examples—the South Vietnamese Army, maybe, or the Bolivian Foreign Service. About the kindest remark that is ever made concerning the efficiency level of the Immigration and Naturalization Service is that the agency has been chronically underfinanced and overworked, and that is a remark usually made by an I.N.S. official.

Simply finding out, through the device of a shrewdly timed buttonholing, which examiner is handling which sort of visa applications is valuable in the immigration practice. So is knowing how to find him. When Immigration announced, a couple of years ago, that it was moving into its present building—a building that was previously occupied by a school called the Bunny Land A-Cat-A-Me—a few immigration lawyers immediately went over to check the place out. They studied the layout of the main public room—a large room that looks a bit like a recently modernized bus station—and poked around the area that was to be restricted to those called in for their appointments with immigration examiners. They studied the possibility of access through side doors and emergency exits. Patrick Murphy—who, partly because of his scholarly background and partly because of the resources of Fulbright & Jaworski, has a renowned collection of books and documents relevant to the practice of immigration law—still carries among the papers in his briefcase a blueprint of the Houston District Office of the Immigration and Naturalization Service. "A blueprint of the building is the key to the practice of immigration law," he told me that rainy Wednesday.

"I beg to differ," a colleague said. "The key to the practice of immigration law is knowing that an immigration examiner who wants to go to the bathroom has to pass through the waiting room to get there."

The process of, say, transforming the holder of a tourist visa or a student visa into a permanent resident of the United States— what laymen call getting a green card—is referred to by lawyers as an adjustment of status. They talk a lot about adjusting people ("I adjusted that Chinese chemist last Wednesday"); a stranger who overheard immigration lawyers discussing visas might think he was listening to chiropractors discussing sacroiliacs. He would be even more likely to think he had stumbled across a crowd of federal bureaucrats—the people immigration lawyers spend most of their time dealing with. Immigration lawyers may talk to one another about the backlog on the I-130s or about who's handling the I-129Bs. It is said that Sam Williamson, gradually becoming more and more frustrated while standing in line inside the immigration office one day, suddenly shouted, "If Jesus tried to get into this country, they'd exclude him on a 212(a)(15)!" Section 212(a) (15) of the Immigration and Nationality Act permits the exclusion of an alien who is likely to become a public charge. Immigration lawyers tell the story as an illustration of Sam Williamson's temperament; they end it by saying that when Timothy Seo, a lawyer of Korean descent, looked astonished at the outburst Williamson thrust a finger toward him and said, "Buddha, too!" It doesn't seem to occur to them that there is anything odd about a man shouting "212(a)(15)" in anger.

"There are about thirty lawyers in Houston who do strictly immigration law and about thirty who do it fifty per cent of their

practice," Patrick Murphy told me one morning while he and I
and Beaumont Martin were standing in line outside Immigration.
"And the rest are a danger to their clients."

"Some of the original thirty are a danger to their clients," Martin said.

Twenty years ago, the national professional organization for
immigration lawyers had one member from Texas—Sam Williamson. The appearance of a few dozen colleagues was not a result of
the increase in undocumented workers coming across the Mexican border. Very few Houston immigration lawyers have a significant number of Mexican clients. When undocumented workers
are picked up, the Immigration Service encourages them to accept
a sort of plea bargain that is known as "voluntary departure"—
returning to their home country with no record of illegal entry or
deportation. Almost all the Mexicans do. Posting bond and going
through a deportation hearing is expensive and difficult; coming
back across the border in a few days usually isn't.

The immigration bar, which was once a phenomenon of the
East Coast, grew all over the country after the immigration policy of the United States changed, in the mid-sixties, from a system
of quotas based on national origin to a rather more complicated
system, which gives preference to reuniting families and filling jobs that American citizens are not available for. It grew dramatically in Houston partly because Houston grew dramatically.
Houston now has any number of multinational corporations that
are constantly transferring executives. It has huge hospitals that
need nurses and technicians. It has colleges that attract foreign
students who don't want to go home when they graduate. It has
substantial ethnic communities, full of people who want to bring
their relatives to this country. Before the changes in the law made
in the sixties, natives of India were virtually excluded from the
United States; Frank Halim estimates that there are now twenty
to twenty-five thousand of them in Houston.

Various lawyers in Houston get various slices of the immigration-law business. Large corporations often take their intra-
company-transfer matters to Charles Foster, who has been the

national president of the American Immigration Lawyers Association and who has his office in one of the new Houston skyscrap-
ers, and who even has a couple of young lawyers in the firm he can
send to the line outside Immigration. Poor Mexicans facing deportation hearings or poor Salvadorans hoping to be granted asylum are often represented by one of the nonprofit organizations
that grew out of the legal-services movement. A lot of Indians go
to Frank Halim, but the division of clients is not strictly along ethnic lines. Corporations that do not retain Charles Foster might
retain Harry Gee, a Chinese-American lawyer who speaks with a
Texas accent. Beaumont Martin may have more Chinese clients
than any of the first-generation Chinese lawyers who can speak
one of the Chinese dialects. Martin is hard pressed to explain that,
except to say that as a lover of Chinese food he figured the best way
to start in the field was to spend a lot of his time hanging around
a café called the Cathay House waiting to be asked if he knew of a
good immigration lawyer.

Sam Williamson could be spotted as a lawyer across the room,
particularly if he happened to be speaking. Williamson—a
short, dapper man with white hair and a full white mustache—
speaks standing up. He might start a conversation sitting down, but
anything more serious than a few exchanges about the weather is
likely to bring him out of his chair. He uses his hands to help form
his sentences. When he is angry, he punches the air with his index
finger. He is usually angry. Luis Wilmot, a young Chicano lawyer
who was instrumental in extending free legal services in Houston
to immigration law, has said, with some admiration, "Sam's got the
longest index finger in town."

Williamson's father was an immigrant named Solomon Wishneweski, who tried farming for a while in a Texas project designed to bring Jews back to the land, and ended up as a railroad
worker in Illinois. He took the name Williamson from the plaque
on a railway engine. Sam Williamson, now in his seventies, still
seems to be a Wishneweski at heart. "It comes natural for a Jew
to become an immigration lawyer," he told me. "There's some-

thing vestigial, something in your blood. We've been strangers so long we resent it."

Williamson is not the sort of lawyer who lays out options and invites the client to take his choice. "People suffer!" he said to me. "I tell them, 'You have a right to be here! You're a living person! You probably got an American kid!' A thing has to be right, not just legal!" Williamson's approach is based partly on his beliefs—that people can't really be divided up between homeborn and strangers, for instance, and that token enforcement of the immigration laws is all that was ever intended. ("The bosses don't want strict enforcement; immigrants represent cheap labor.") It is also an approach that is probably inevitable for a man of his nature. "I like to scrap," he says. "I come in slugging."

When I visited Williamson in his office one afternoon, he was irritated about a suspension-of-deportation case he was handling. An immigration judge can suspend an order of deportation if the alien involved can demonstrate that he has lived continuously in the United States for at least seven years, that he is of good moral character, and that being deported would cause "extreme hardship." The alien's lawyer may try to demonstrate that children who were born in this country (and are therefore citizens, whatever the status of their parents) would suffer cultural displacement or psychological damage by being moved to a country that they have never known. The judge is rarely convinced that the hardship being demonstrated is extreme. Williamson figures he has tried about a hundred suspension cases and won perhaps five. He wasn't optimistic about winning the one he was working on. "Some poor bastard has been here eleven years," he said. "His wife's a permanent resident. You ought to hear them down there rank gradations of hardship! The bastards! I could tear them apart!"

As a former English professor, Patrick Murphy is among a number of Houston immigration lawyers who used to be in another line of work. Frank Halim, for instance, was a lobbyist for the wholesale grocers' association. George Sellnau, who is the chairman of the Texas chapter of the American Immigration Lawyers

Association, was for many years a metallurgist. Even people who grow up wanting to be lawyers do not ordinarily aspire to the practice of immigration law. In the Southwest, the practice is sometimes associated in the public mind with people who advertise that they can fix papers or people who sell immigrants a worthless piece of paper that is said to constitute a *"permiso."* Immigration lawyers would point out that such people normally are not in fact members of the bar. Immigration lawyers would also acknowledge that there are members of the bar who exploit aliens—people willing to collect monthly fees, for instance, for doing nothing on cases that offer no chance of a successful conclusion anyway. Even the reputable practice of immigration law is not thought of as an exalted form of the profession. "There has always been an image problem," Charles Foster told me. "The immigration bar has always teetered between a profession and a visa-application service."

The only immigration lawyer in Houston who must have considered immigration law as a career since childhood is Peter Williamson, who is Sam Williamson's son. Even he started out in another area of law—as an attorney for the farm workers' union. Peter Williamson is thought to have inherited some of his father's contentiousness. A year and a half ago, when he became frustrated at his inability to get any information from Immigration about cases that had been delayed for years, he began going to Federal District Court and filing for writs of mandamus that would have forced I.N.S. officials to act. "They hate to get sued," Pete Williamson says, with a certain satisfaction. Some of his colleagues think that his willingness to go to court was what forced the district office to institute a system by which each lawyer, in turn, is permitted to bring five exceptionally old cases to the personal attention of the deputy director. Sam Williamson, who complains that most of his fellow immigration lawyers are namby-pamby, sometimes makes a grudging exception of his son. "Oh, there's some hint in Peter that he grew up in my house," he told me.

"Have you ever won a suspension case?" I asked an immigration lawyer in Houston.

"It depends on what you mean by winning," he said.

Immigration lawyers win time. Given calendar delays and court appeals and bureaucratic lethargy, a suspension-of-deportation action might take years. The immigration judges in Houston have almost never granted asylum to a Salvadoran, so, strictly speaking, lawyers in Houston have almost never won a Salvadoran-asylum case. On the other hand, there is a backlog of eight thousand asylum cases to be heard in Houston, there are only two immigration judges to hear them, and there are three levels of appeal—so, speaking not very strictly, lawyers have won a lot of time in Salvadoran-asylum cases. In time, as immigration lawyers say, "something good could happen." The client might marry a citizen—giving him permanent-resident status unless Immigration decides that the marriage is a sham. The client might find a job that makes it possible to get permanent residence through labor certification. Congress might pass the Simpson-Mazzoli bill, which would legalize the presence of any alien who can demonstrate that he has lived in this country since before some specified date. The I.N.S. might lose the file. Meanwhile, the client is in the United States, and that is what he wanted in the first place. Nothing good is likely to happen to someone who is hanging around the American consulate in Karachi or Salonika waiting for an immigrant visa—one reason that, in the words of George Sellnau, "any immigration lawyer worth his salt would say, 'Get here first!'"

The fact that an alien has been living in the United States for months, or even years, with no more documentation than an expired student visa does not prevent him from getting a green card if, say, he manages to get labor certification before Immigration manages to deport him. One reason that lawyers are so eager to grab an immigration examiner as he walks through the waiting room is that they are often trying to juggle matters in a way that makes something good happen before something bad happens. Immigration lawyers are people who have an interest in seeing that some folders are on the top of the pile and some folders are on the bottom of the pile.

When Patrick Murphy, of Fulbright & Jaworski, feels the need to consult a colleague, he often calls Beaumont Martin. They became well acquainted standing outside Immigration on Wednesday mornings. Once, finding themselves with time on their hands in the waiting room of Immigration, they collaborated with Ed Prud'homme and a lawyer named Sana Loue on a reading of "Hamlet"—a reading whose best dramatic effects were presumably lost on the Vietnamese boat people and Salvadoran refugees who make up a good part of the waiting-room audience. "He's a very intelligent man," Murphy says of Martin. "He just marches to a different drummer."

Martin is quick to acknowledge being out of step. "When clients refer people to me, they say, 'He's a strange guy, so don't be put off by his personality,'" he told me. Martin finds that reasonable advice. When he came to Houston, some twenty years ago, a friend recommended a dentist, and thought to mention that Martin should not be put off by the dentist's singing. "There I was in the chair waiting for him to come in, frightened already," Martin told me, "and I heard a man outside the door singing." Martin began to imitate the singing dentist: "'Oh, the dentist is your friend, tra-la-la, the dentist is your friend.'" He paused. "If I hadn't been warned," he went on, "I might have become alarmed."

Potential clients who have not been warned are sometimes alarmed by Martin's jumpsuits or his office. He shares a small brick building with the singing dentist on an otherwise rundown street close to Houston's medical complex. It is not a neat office. Martin has a desk, but he tends to sit in a lounge chair and pile papers on the floor next to him. The office is filled with souvenirs—a fat-tummied little Buddha, a huge walking stick, an ersatz armor breastplate. Martin likes to bring things back from trips, and he likes to send away for things. He is often hot on the trail of something through the mail—a ketchup-making kit, or a phonograph record that someone in England made by tape-recording the noises of sheep and arranging them into a song ("Flock Around the Clock"). He is equally intent on local investigations, such as a search for a supermarket having a sale on York Peppermint Patties, one of his favorite foods. The dominant design element of Martin's office is provided by statues of bare-breasted women. Apparently, some client brought Martin one of the statues as a souvenir, and then he started getting bare-breasted women from everyone, the way some people with collections are always brought pipes or porcelain animals. Someone also brought him a sign that says "BOOB NUT!"

Martin is a man in his late forties with slicked-back hair and an intense gaze and a way of enunciating each syllable distinctly. He is married to a nurse from the Philippines. He was brought up in Washington, and while he was working as a lawyer for the federal government he asked for a transfer to Houston in order to get out of his home town. When he decided to go into private practice, some sort of federal administrative law seemed natural, and people around the hospital complex provided the core of an immigration practice. Ed Prud'homme describes Martin's practice this way: "Beaumont takes nice, clean cases with no funny Joneses in them."

Martin does not have any of the corporate business that is generally an immigration lawyer's most lucrative trade—I suspect that Houston corporation executives tend not to patronize singing dentists, either—but he also avoids the least profitable cases, like deportation hearings. While I was in the office one day, he met with a Turkish waiter who had married an American citizen, an Egyptian who was getting a green card for his twelve-year-old daughter, and two Chinese students who had come to Houston and were now trying to get their green cards through labor certification. The process of getting labor certification amounts to staging a sort of sham employment offer. The lawyer writes a job description that complies with the Department of Labor's standards, and the potential employer of the alien actually advertises such a job through the state employment commission. If someone shows up who is a citizen and has the qualifications outlined in the ad and is willing to work for the stated wage, the labor certification is not granted—although the employer has no obligation to give the citizen a job. If the lawyer who wrote the job description has been skillful, there is a good chance that no qualified citizen will show up. Writing job descriptions that pass the Department of Labor but attract no other potential employees is what Ed Prud'homme calls "one of the few art forms in the business," and Beaumont Martin is considered one of the artists. One of the Chinese students had managed to get a job in the accounting department of a small oil company, and, since the job required some computer expertise, Martin decided to write a job description that nudged her over a bit from accounting to computer analysis. ("There are a lot of people running around with accounting degrees.") When he had typed it up, he handed it to her:

SYSTEMS ANALYST 020.067-018

Conduct analyses of accounting, management, and operational problems and formulate mathematical models for solution by IBM computer system, using FORTRAN, COBOL, and PAS-CAL. Analyze problems in terms of management information. Write computer programs and devise and install accounting system and related procedures. Masters or equal in management information systems. $1667/month.

She read it over. "It's beautiful," she said.

In his waiting room, Martin keeps a supply of brochures that answer questions about immigration law and list his fees—somewhat lower than those of most lawyers in town. For Martin's work in acquiring a green card for her through labor certification, the Chinese student would pay nine hundred dollars. Martin often tells people who come in for less artistic procedures that they don't really need a lawyer. ("You could do it yourself—I'll even give you the forms. If I do it, I'll charge you six hundred dollars.") His brochure says, "If you have consulted me and decide that you do not want me to represent you, don't ruin my day by telling me. Smile, pay the consultation fee, and leave." Apparently, most people stay. Martin's approach is based on carrying a high volume of cases, and he seems to do that. Some immigration lawyers do quite well financially, and there is a widespread feeling among the members of the bar who wait outside Immigration that Beaumont Martin, working without a secretary or a necktie, makes more money than any other immigration lawyer in Houston.

Unlike Charles Foster, Martin does not worry much about whether immigration law is taken seriously as a profession ("I'm a paper pusher, not a lawyer"); unlike such people as Sam Williamson, he does not see his practice as a cause ("They have an attitude that is based on a noble concept of the profession, and I just don't have it"). Martin says that he sees his practice as "a vehicle for me to support my life style." He says that it is often mundane and repetitious. "I hear my colleagues talk about these fascinating cases," he told me. "My cases are generally not fascinating. Maybe it's the office. Maybe they wouldn't trust me with a fascinating case. I might say it was simple, and they'd figure that meant I was too stupid to understand it."

"We do nothing but deportation work here," Luis Wilmot told me. "And we're going out of business." When Wilmot helped establish legal services for poor people in Houston who had immigration problems, he was with a legal-services agency called the Gulf Coast Legal Foundation. While I was in Houston, both he and the one other immigration lawyer at Gulf Coast were about to leave for other jobs. A sort of spinoff immigration-law center that Gulf Coast organized still exists, and so do a couple of other nonprofit organizations in the field; they have all been forced to start charging small fees, though, and there is some question whether they can operate at a volume that will allow them to survive. The free legal service offered to immigrants by Gulf Coast will end partly because of fund cutbacks but mostly because guidelines handed down by the federal Legal Services Corporation severely restrict the sort of aliens who can be taken on as clients. Although the guidelines are complicated, Wilmot can state in one phrase his interpretation of which clients they eliminate: "the people who need the most help."

There are several private lawyers in Houston who represent poor Mexicans and Central Americans. A few of them have legal services backgrounds; Wilmot's response to the mention of one or two of the others is a silent shudder. The local chapter of the American Immigration Lawyers Association has anticipated that some of its members will be taking some deportation cases on a pro-bono basis. The sort of cases that may turn out not to be handled by anyone, legal-services lawyers think, are those which have to do with the general rights of aliens. What is known as the Alien School Case, for instance—the case in which the Supreme Court ruled that the children of undocumented aliens could not be prohibited from attending Texas public schools—was brought by legal-services lawyers. Although the Houston lawyers with legal-services backgrounds think of most private immigration lawyers in town as "pro-immigrant," they also think that most private immigration lawyers "don't want to rock the boat down at Immigration."

Private lawyers tend to think that the system for admitting immigrants to the United States is not well run; legal-services lawyers tend to think that it is basically unfair. They think that it is unfair to treat Mexico, a country that shares a two-thousand-mile border with the United States, "as if it were Luxembourg." They believe that it is unfair to give asylum to a Russian ballerina who faces no persecution at home that she did not provoke by defecting, and not give asylum to a Salvadoran refugee who has a fair chance of getting killed in El Salvador. It is accepted among immigration lawyers that a request for asylum—a request that, by law, must be based on a well-founded belief on the part of the alien that returning to his homeland would cause him to be persecuted for his politics or his religion or his associates—is much more likely to be granted if the homeland in question has a government that the State Department considers to be in the camp of the wicked. (Salvadorans whose most fervent desire is to stay in the United States permanently are presumably rooting for the guerrillas.) Legal-services lawyers tend to have a sympathy for Salvadoran refugees which is based on political as well as humane considerations—on the belief, for instance, that Central Americans have been forced to seek refuge partly because the United States has propped up dictatorial regimes that do not have the support of the people. "The United States is not an innocent party," Luis Wilmot says.

One of the procedures that Beaumont Martin often tells potential clients that they can carry out themselves is filing for a green card on the basis of having married an American citizen. If they are good at English and uncowed by bureaucrats, they might indeed file the papers themselves—although they might stand in line for hours, present documents to the clerk at the counter, and be told, perhaps not terribly politely, that some mistake or omission means that they have to go through the process all over again another day. Also, immigration lawyers can predict a good number of the questions an immigration examiner is likely to ask if he has reason to suspect that the marriage is a sham: Where does she put her shoes at night? What do his parents do for a living? What's his favorite food? Where did you meet her?

A lawyer is not allowed to coach his clients during the interview, but his presence can provide not just a sense of security but a sort of implied character witness. An immigration lawyer's practice depends to some extent on his reputation at Immigration, so it is obviously not in his best interest to become known as someone who shows up in the company of couples he suspects are attached only by the requirements necessary for a green card. Immigration examiners, many of whom began their career as border patrolmen, tend to be suspicious by nature, and most of them have seen their suspicions confirmed any number of times. True love hit Iranian students with a peculiar frequency a few years ago, when a lot of them had visa problems; Nigerian students are also known for being quick down the aisle. Any couple who seem far apart culturally or ethnically or linguistically obviously raise suspicions, even if they are accompanied by a pillar of the immigration bar. When the Turkish waiter Beaumont Martin was representing showed up with his new American wife outside Immigration one Wednesday, she turned out to be a nice-looking, exceedingly dark-skinned black woman. Ed Prud'homme looked the couple over, turned to Martin, and said, in the shorthand that allows old acquaintances to place bets with each other without much elaboration, "Three dollars."

Along with the forms and folders on the floor next to Beaumont Martin's lounge chair was a worn copy of a fourteen-hundred-page government book called Dictionary of Occupational Titles—known to immigration lawyers as the D.O.T. For anyone who wants to make labor certification into an art form, the D.O.T. is an essential piece of equipment. It contains one-paragraph descriptions of virtually every occupation practiced by anybody in the United States. It describes the task of a neurosurgeon and it describes the task of a fibre-glass-container-winding operator. In a consistently direct style, it says what a leak hunter does ("Inspects barrels filled with beer or whisky to detect and repair leaking barrels") and what a sponge buffer does ("Tends machine that buffs edges of household sponges to impart rounded finish") and what an airline pilot does ("Pilots airplane"). Using the D.O.T. as a guide, an immigration lawyer tries to give the client an occupational title in the least crowded field available and then describe the job in a paragraph that sounds pretty much like a paragraph in the D.O.T. but happens to describe almost nobody but the client in question. "Immigration law is taking a short-order cook and making him into an executive chef," Pete Williamson told me. "What we're talking about here is a matter of focus."

When I was discussing labor certification with Pete Williamson one afternoon, he mentioned a young woman he had seen that day who wanted to stay in the country but did not fall into any of the categories of family reunification. She obviously did not qualify for any of the non-immigrant visas available to businessmen or investors. She was already married—to someone who, as it happened, had more or less the same visa problems that she did. Her only hope for a green card was labor certification. Her only occupation was looking after the children of a neighbor.

I said that it didn't sound promising. A few days with immigration lawyers had greatly broadened my view of how the employ-

ment sections of the immigration law were actually used. I was
no longer under the delusion that the law worked to bring to this
country people who had rare skills or worked in fields where there
were serious shortages of American workers. "It's a matter of
nudging the client's situation over a bit one way or another in order to make it fit into a category that's eligible," one lawyer had told
me. "And sometimes, if you want to stay in the United States, you
have to shape your career to fit the immigration law." Williamson
had explained that it was possible for, say, a South American shirt
manufacturer who wanted to resettle here to come in on a visitor's
visa or a business visa, establish a corporation, have the person-
nel department of the corporation file an application to have him
labor-certified as the president of a shirt firm doing business with
Latin America ("Must know Spanish. Must be familiar with South
American cottons . . ."), apply for a green card through the labor
certification, and settle in for life. Still, it seemed unlikely that being a mother's helper in Texas was a job "for which a shortage of
employable and willing persons exists."

There were two other important elements in the case, Williamson said. The young woman in question was a college graduate.
Also, both she and the children she looked after were Muslims—
all from Pakistan. Williamson intended to nudge her over from a
nanny to a tutor—a tutor qualified to instruct the children in their
own culture and religion. He thought it unlikely that any citizen
with similar qualifications would respond to the ad. Williamson
takes some satisfaction in such focussing—enough, he says, to
offset the repetitiousness of certain aspects of the practice and
the frustrations of dealing with the Immigration and Naturalization Service. "It's a competent, involved, technical job in which, if
you're successful, you can see the consequences of your actions,"
he told me when I asked what appealed to him about practicing
immigration law. "Also, I don't like the government."

A sking immigration lawyers what they don't like about the
practice of immigration law amounts to requesting an ad-
dress on the evils of the Immigration and Naturalization Service.

Immigration lawyers talk about the I.N.S. with the intensity that people reserve for discussing institutions that dominate their lives. For most immigration lawyers in Houston, Immigration is the only adversary they face and the only judge they petition. Their connection with Immigration is the connection that permits them to ply their trade and the connection that sometimes makes them wonder if they have gone into the right trade after all. The significant favors that are bestowed upon them are bestowed by Immigration. The most devastating disservices done to them are done by Immigration. For an immigration lawyer, Immigration is the enemy and Immigration is the benefactor—and which one it is going to be on any given day often seems to be a matter of whimsy. When immigration lawyers in Houston want to kid one another—sometimes with a bit of an edge—the form that the kidding often takes is an accusation of being a sycophant at Immigration.

Charles Foster, a friendly, energetic man in his early forties, has the style and accoutrements of a successful downtown lawyer. His firm is in one of the modern Houston towers that have the equivalent of designer labels to distinguish them from the off-the-rack office buildings—architecture by Pei, in this case, and plaza sculpture by Miró. His office furnishings include an antique sideboard and a picture of himself with the governor and diplomas from the University of Texas and a picture of himself with John Glenn, whose campaign he served as co-chairman of Texas Attorneys for John Glenn. For lunch, he often walks over to a nearby office building that has on its top floor an attorneys' luncheon club called the Inns of Court.

As someone who had always been interested in foreign affairs, Foster decided as an undergraduate that he would go into international law—a field that he later realized did not have as much to do with the great issues of public policy as an undergraduate might imagine. He began his career in the international section of a large Wall Street firm, and returned to Houston in the late sixties to join a large downtown firm—about the time the change in national immigration policy began to present the opportunities that eventually convinced him he should go out on his own with a specialty in immigration law. Foster likes the client contact involved in the immigration practice—on Wall Street, he had been practicing for six months before he laid eyes on a client—but he laments the fact that a lot of clients, having come from countries where documents are acquired by quiet exchanges of cash, regard immigration lawyers as fixers rather than as professionals. "I had one client, from the Middle East, and I was explaining to him through an interpreter that his case was a very complicated and difficult one," Foster told me. "Finally, the interpreter stopped me and said, 'Mr. So-and-So will pay your fee.' It was hard to make them understand that I wasn't trying to get more money to bribe someone."

When some commission wants to know the opinion of attorneys about immigration policy, Charles Foster is usually one of the people asked. In his day-to-day practice, though, he is no more concerned with the great issues of public policy than he would be if he were an international lawyer giving an opinion on whether or not a particular corporation was operating in conformity with the zoning laws of a foreign country. "What I do is take a bunch of diverse facts and put them into a pattern in a way that will fit into the statutory system," he says. An attorney is normally hired not to decide what is fair or what is in the public interest but to decide what is possible. "Often, people come in here and tell me they would like to sponsor the person they've brought in," Foster said. "And they start telling me what a wonderful addition to the country he'd make and what a fine, upstanding man he is. And I listen, because I think it's good to have those things said. But what I'm doing while he talks is listening for the technicalities."

Lately, the monthly get-togethers of the Houston immigration bar have been held in the cocktail lounge of the Tokyo Gardens restaurant, just down the street from the Galleria shopping center. They are usually jolly events. Immigration lawyers in Houston tend to get along. They routinely trade information—what new questions examiners are asking to test for sham marriages, for instance, or how some document that is easily obtained can satisfy the requirement for one that is always difficult to get. They have a variety of viewpoints concerning the practice, of course. Sam Williamson says immigration law divides into cases and procedures, and leaves no doubt about which he considers the higher calling. Beaumont Martin, whose practice is made up almost exclusively of what Williamson would call procedures, says Williamson "wants to take every case to the Supreme Court." Charles Foster says he admires Beaumont Martin but makes no secret of being relieved that most members of the Houston immigration bar practice law more conventionally and wear more conventional clothing while doing it.

At the gathering I attended, Ed Prud'homme found out that he had not in fact won three dollars on the outcome of the Turkish waiter's interview. Beaumont Martin acknowledged, though, that the questioning had been unusually prolonged. The waiter, he reported, had almost destroyed his own case when he seemed to avoid giving a specific answer about the last gift he had received from his wife. Before the waiter was in the room, his wife had answered the same question by saying that she had given him some undershorts; apparently, he was embarrassed to mention such intimate apparel before strangers. "I finally started laughing," Martin said. "So did the examiner. It was so much like 'The Newlywed Game.'"

The business meeting, chaired by George Sellnau, was dominated by a discussion of relations with Immigration—particularly concerning the special line for lawyers. Someone had been at the district office one morning that week when there was a scuffle between the gate guard and an out-of-town lawyer who thought he had a right to enter a public building. Someone else had been present when an Iranian who was handling his own case complained loudly that the two lawyers ahead of him in line at the clerk's window had not been in the line outside. Someone had been present when there were complaints outside Immigration that lawyers were being allowed through the gate while old people and women with babies remained outside in the cold. The discussion reflected the realization by everyone in the room that even skill at an art form like labor certification was not as important to an immigration lawyer as simple access to the district office. A lawyer named William Sim, who had that very week heard an I.N.S. official say something that made him think the entire system was in danger of being scrapped, summed up his response to that prospect in one sentence: "I had the feeling the sky fell down."

—1984

PRESIDENTIAL UPS AND DOWNS

Washington Pundits Take Their Analytical Skills to the Ranch

CRAWFORD, TEX., AUG. 20—President George W. Bush's failure to catch a fish after he spent two hours on his heavily stocked bass pond this afternoon was considered a defeat for Mr. Bush by most observers here, and one that would weaken his position in swapping fish stories with Democrats and Republican moderates in Congress. A White House spokesman's comment that the President, being a serious conservationist, had "done catch-and-release one better" may have only worsened matters, since most of the press corps dismissed it as a desperate attempt at spin.

CRAWFORD, TEX., AUG. 21—The President scored a solid victory today by working on the clearing of his nature trail for an hour and a half without injuring himself.

CRAWFORD, TEX., AUG. 22—Eating scrambled eggs this morning for breakfast was seen as a victory for the President, who had been having his eggs sunny-side up for more than a week. The President prefers his eggs scrambled. White House officials have been unwilling to discuss the reasoning behind the apparently contradictory sunny-side-up policy. However, they are not directly denying a story that the Crawford ranch's cook, Rosa Gonzales, had refused to serve scrambled eggs ever since the President, in an effort to compliment her, tried to pronounce the dish in Spanish—*huevos revueltos*—and came out with something that Ms. Gonzales understood as "very revolting." It is not clear how the situation was resolved in a manner that permitted a return to scrambled eggs this morning, but White House officials did little to hide their jubilation.

CRAWFORD, TEX., AUG. 23—White House spokesmen refused to elaborate on a terse announcement this morning that a two-year-old Hereford steer on the Bush ranch had stepped into a gopher hole and broken its leg—a defeat for the President.

CRAWFORD, TEX., AUG. 24—Even George W. Bush's harshest critics are acknowledging today that the weather has given the President an important victory. "The entire country has been suffering from a heat wave," said a member of the White House staff who has been at the President's ranch for three weeks, "but there can't be any place quite as miserable as this." Daniel Jonas, a Democratic pollster who specializes in issues of empathy, said, "Let's face it: this is a big one for Bush."

CRAWFORD, TEX., AUG. 25—George W. Bush was served *huevos rancheros* for breakfast today—a serious defeat for the President, who does not like highly spiced food.

CRAWFORD, TEX., AUG. 26—Republicans both here and in Washington were glowing today after George W. Bush apparently scored a big victory by losing at golf. "He's just a regular guy with a bad slice," one Party loyalist said. "He knows loss. He understands loss." The low scorer in the foursome, a wealthy oilman from Lubbock, won ten dollars from each of the other players. Late this afternoon, Democrats were saying that the episode might prove to be a defeat for Mr. Bush now that it is known that longtime family friends of the President's parents came forward on the eighteenth green to cover his losses.

CRAWFORD, TEX., AUG. 27—President Bush scored his biggest victory of the week this morning when Rosa Gonzales, his cook, posed, smiling, for a picture with him in the kitchen of the Crawford ranch. Although Ms. Gonzales has not been made available for interviews, the White House has formally denied that she ever referred to the President as *"la boquita de un gringo puro"*—roughly, "little gringo mouth." In response to reporters' questions at the photo opportunity, the President explained his views on how best to prepare eggs by saying that he is a uniter, not a divider. H. Cole Knudnik, an expert on Presidential diet at the Brookings Institution, said, "The President was overdue for a clear-cut victory on this one, and he got it."

—2001

THE LIFE AND TIMES OF
JOE BOB BRIGGS, SO FAR

The problem was how to deal with trashy movies. It's a common problem among movie reviewers. What, exactly, does the film critic of a main-line American daily newspaper do about movies like "The Night Evelyn Came Out of the Grave" and "Malibu Hot Summer" and "Bloodsucking Freaks"? Does he pick one out, on a slow week, and subject it to the sort of withering sarcasm that sometimes, in his braver daydreams, he sees himself using on the executive editor? Does he simply ignore such movies, preferring to pretend that a person of his sensibilities could not share an artistic universe with such efforts as "Mother Riley Meets the Vampire" and "Driller Killer" and "Gas Pump Girls"?

The Dallas *Times Herald* had that problem, and in late 1981 it seemed to have more or less stumbled onto a solution. The assistant managing editor for features, Ron Smith, had asked the movie reviewer, a young man named John Bloom, to look into the question of why drive-in movie theatres, which were folding in most places, still thrived in patches of the country that included the area around Dallas. Bloom came back with a proposal: He could review the sort of movies that play in Texas drive-ins—they are sometimes called exploitation movies—through the persona of a fictional drive-in customer who was actually able to distinguish between a successful zombie-surfing movie and a zombie-surfing movie that didn't quite work. "I had been thinking about doing a column from someone with a personality that is completely opposite of what we think is tasteful," Bloom recalled not long ago. "I had been saying to Ron, 'What would happen if a movie critic loved "I Spit on Your Grave" and hated "Dumbo"? What if this guy suddenly had an aesthetic revelation and started looking at Charles Bronson as an *auteur*?'"

Bloom first suggested a reviewer named Bobo Rodriguez. He

envisioned Bobo as a "kind of all-purpose ethnic, like Andy Kauf-
man's foreigner: you don't know what nationality he is but he's
quintessentially foreign." Smith rejected Bobo Rodriguez as a
character Dallas minorities were bound to find offensive no matter how many times they were assured that the real target was
pretentious film criticism or respectable Anglo moviegoers. The
character Bloom came up with instead was a young redneck he
called Joe Bob Briggs. Smith liked that idea. He decided to give Joe
Bob some space in the back pages of *Weekend,* the paper's Friday
entertainment tabloid—a low-priority operation that was generally avoided by reporters and was probably best known to readers as the part of the *Times Herald* most likely to come off on your
hands. In January of 1982, the *Times Herald* ran Joe Bob Briggs'
first movie review, under the heading "Joe Bob Goes to the Drive-
In." The movie being considered was "The Grim Reaper," in which
the title character "likes to kill people and then chew on them for a
while." Joe Bob liked it.

In an accompanying piece introducing his new colleague to the
readers of the *Times Herald,* John Bloom said he had met Joe Bob
at the snack bar of the Century Drive-In, in Grand Prairie, Texas,
during an all-night Bela Lugosi marathon. According to Bloom,
Joe Bob was, at nineteen, a drive-in authority of enormous experience: he had seen sixty-eight hundred drive-in movies, and had
still found time for at least three marriages. Experience had not
brought a strong sense of responsibility. Only a month or so after the column began—a month during which John Bloom found
a Brazilian film called "Pixote" to be "powerful" and "unsettling,"
and Joe Bob praised not only "Mad Monkey Kung Fu" ("We're
talking serious chopsocky here") but a snakebite horror movie
that his girlfriend of the moment, May Ellen Masters, refused
to watch with her eyes open—the new columnist disappeared.
(Bloom had taken some vacation time.) Bloom finally reported
that he had found Joe Bob—in jail, in Bossier City, Louisiana. Joe
Bob had been arrested for beating up an auto mechanic named
Gus Simpson, who not only had sold Joe Bob's baby-blue Dodge
Dart for parts to Junior Stebbens, of Mineral Wells, but also had

been discovered by Joe Bob with the perfidious May Ellen Masters in a room at the Have-A-Ball Tourist Courts. By that time, it was clear from the volume of inquiries about Joe Bob's whereabouts that "Joe Bob Goes to the Drive-In," which Smith had envisioned as an occasional feature, or maybe even a onetime event, had become a Friday staple of the *Times Herald*.

Eventually, Bloom's authorship became a sort of open secret in the Dallas newspaper world, but for the better part of a year it was a real secret even from the people who worked in the *Times Herald* newsroom. A lot of readers believed that the Joe Bob Briggs column was in fact written by a nineteen-year-old redneck who had seen sixty-eight hundred drive-in movies. "They bought that," Ron Smith said recently, sounding amazed as he recalled it. "There were people on this staff—serious newspaper people—who bought that." Many of those who finally became suspicious, of course, settled their suspicions on John Bloom. He was, after all, the only person on the paper who claimed to have met Joe Bob. He was the movie reviewer. His initials were similar to Joe Bob's initials. Close readers might have even noticed that when Bloom wrote about Joe Bob in those first weeks of shepherding the column into the paper he fell into rather Joe Bobbian phrasing himself—as when he wrote that Joe Bob's adventures around Bossier City had left his head looking like "the inside of a Big Mac after it's been left on the dashboard three or four days," or when he wrote that Joe Bob's previous car had been ruined at the Ark-La-Tex Twin "when a dough-head in a Barracuda crunched his rear door and scared Dede Wilks half out of her halter top." Bloom's basic defense against the accusations of authorship was that he could hardly have been less like Joe Bob. A soft-spoken, reserved, almost withdrawn young man who had graduated with honors from Vanderbilt, Bloom drove a Toyota instead of a baby-blue 1968 Dodge Dart. He spoke with a trace of Southwestern accent, but it would have been difficult to imagine him using Joe Bobbisms like "He don't give a diddly" or expressing his admiration for an actress by saying, "Bootsie is not just another humongous set of garbanzas." An admirer of foreign films, Bloom wrote essays on the *nouvelle vague* while Joe Bob was rating movies according to the amount of innards displayed ("We're talking Glopola City") and the number of severed body parts that can be seen rolling away and the number of breasts exposed ("the garbanza department").

Bloom wanted Joe Bob to "talk about movies the way most people talk about movies: they give the plot, with emphasis on their favorite scenes, then they sum up what they think of it." Joe Bob tended to tell the plot ("So this flick starts off with a bimbo getting chained up and killed by a bunch of Meskins dressed up like Roman soldiers in their bathrobes"), and his summaries eventually developed into his best-known trademark: "Sixty-four dead bodies. Bimbos in cages. Bimbos in chains. Arms roll. Thirty-nine breasts. Two beasts (giant lizard, octopus). Leprosy. Kung fu. Bimbo fu. Sword fu. Lizard fu. Knife fu. Seven battles. Three quarts blood. A 39 on the vomit meter . . . Joe Bob says check it out."

What some readers wondered about such material was not who was writing it but how it got into the newspaper. The short answer was that it was sneaked in. Ron Smith and Bloom, playing around with ways to handle a section of the paper that even the editors didn't read very closely, hadn't taken the Joe Bob gimmick seriously enough as a long-term proposition to consult any of the sort of editors Joe Bob began referring to in print as high sheriffs. If a gathering of top editors had been presented with a formal plan to run a truly tasteless weekly column by a fictional trash-movie fanatic, Joe Bob Briggs would presumably have gone the way of Bobo Rodriguez. The Dallas *Times Herald* was a lively newspaper, but even lively newspapers are cautious institutions. As it was, the Joe Bob column impressed itself on the consciousness of the paper's principal editors after it had begun gaining a foothold with the readers. Not long after that, it became apparent that "Joe Bob Goes to the Drive-In" was on its way to becoming the most talked-about feature in the paper. "You can't imagine what incredible appeal it had in those early months," someone who was at the *Times Herald* at the time said recently. "When the Friday paper came out, everyone in the newsroom stopped whatever he was doing to turn to *Weekend* and find out what outrage Joe Bob was perpetrating now." The same thing was happening all over town. Friday was Joe Bob Day among young professional people who worked in the shiny new office buildings of downtown Dallas. Friday was also Joe Bob Day among folks who, in the words of one *Times Herald* reporter, "were grateful that there was finally someone in the paper who wrote normal."

The top editors of the *Times Herald* were constantly being reassured that the perpetration of outrages was all right. It was satire, they were told; it was not really written by some crazed redneck, after all, but by the thoughtful and enlightened John Bloom. But they were still uneasy about running Joe Bob's column. Daily newspapers have never been comfortable with satire. Daily newspapers have never been comfortable with columnists who perpetrate outrages. Then, in November of 1982, the *Wall Street Journal* ran a long front-page story by G. Christian Hill headlined "AFICIONADO OF TRASH AT THE TIMES HERALD IS A BIG HIT IN DALLAS." The *Journal* piece conferred an almost instant legitimacy on "Joe Bob Goes to the Drive-In." The high sheriffs at the *Times Herald* breathed easier. The Los Angeles Times Syndicate—whose parent company, the Times Mirror Company, owned the Dallas *Times Herald*—offered Joe Bob a syndication contract. A young woman who had met Bloom through handling the advertising for some Dallas exploitation-movie distributors became a literary agent on the spot, and sent a Joe Bob Briggs book proposal to fifty editors whose names she got out of a guide to the publishing industry. Joe Bob wrote the proposal's covering letter himself. Since it was important correspondence, he used his special stationery—the stuff decorated with reproductions of movie posters for drive-in classics like "Doctor Butcher, M.D." and "The Slumber Party Massacre" and "Vampire Playgirls."

The letter began, "Dear Big Shot Publisher: Cherry Dilday is typing this sucker up for me, so if we got technical problems, I'm telling you right now, I'm not responsible. Cherry claims she got a typing diploma from the Industrial Trades Institute on Harry Hines Boulevard, but I know for a fact that she left school after two weeks to go to the dog track in West Memphis with Dexter Crook.

She'd probly amount to something today if she'd stayed for the full three. Correct me if I'm wrong, but I've been told you're interested in getting filthy rich off my book." Several of them were. Joe Bob signed a contract with Dell.

Among large American cities, Dallas has had a reputation for being run, rather smoothly, by an oligarchy. While other cities of the Old Confederacy were battling over the demands of the civil-rights movement, for instance, whatever desegregation could not be avoided in Dallas was arranged quietly from above by a group of conservative white businessmen called the Dallas Citizens Council—a fact often mentioned to explain why Dallas's black community has been slow to develop aggressive and independent leaders of its own. The Citizens Council also installed slates of city councilmen. Jim Schutze, who does an urban-affairs column for the *Times Herald*, has written that until 1978, when city councilmen began being elected in single-member districts instead of at large, Dallas was, in effect, a "well-run predemocratic city-state." The oligarchy's newspaper was the Dallas *Morning News*—an appropriately sober, locally owned, journalistically conservative paper, whose editorial page is even now described occasionally as Dixiecrat. Until a dozen years ago, the *Morning News* dominated the Dallas newspaper market. Its competition, the Dallas *Times Herald*, was an afternoon paper that had a smaller circulation and carried advertising that ran more toward K mart than toward Neiman-Marcus. Like a lot of afternoon papers, the *Times Herald* concentrated on local coverage—particularly the juicier murders. The joke names for the two papers in Dallas were the *Morning Snooze* and the *Crimes Herald*.

In the middle seventies, all that changed. The Times Mirror Company—a huge, expansionist communications corporation whose empire includes the Los Angeles *Times* and *Newsday*—had bought the *Times Herald* in 1969, in a deal that included five-year contracts for the management that was in place. As the contracts expired, the *Times Herald* launched an ambitious campaign to overtake the *Morning News* and become the preëminent newspa-

per of Dallas—a prize of considerable value, since the Dallas market was expanding daily in the Texas boom that had been touched
off by the Arab oil embargo and fed by Sun Belt migration. The
Times Herald gradually transformed itself into an all-day paper.
New editors were hired from papers like the Washington *Post* and
the Philadelphia *Inquirer*, and the new editors brought in eager
young reporters from all over the country. The news coverage was
aggressive, and the editors made it clear that they were unconcerned about which powerful citizen or potential advertiser might
be in the line of fire. A sign on the newsroom wall said, "THE
ONLY SACRED COW HERE IS HAMBURGER." The newsroom
took on the sort of élan that in the early sixties was associated
with the New York *Herald Tribune*. Reporters were encouraged to
come up with stories that had what the new managing editor, Will
Jarrett, called "pop" or "sizzle." The editorial page found a mod-
erate niche in that vast area of opinion that lay to the left of the
Dallas *Morning News*, and it put forward late-twentieth-century
views on racial and social issues. The *Times Herald* solidified its
position as the newspaper that concerned itself with the problems
of Dallas's minorities, but, in a way, the new version of the paper
seemed to be directed toward a new Dallas audience—the people
who had moved to the Sun Belt from the North, the younger Dallas
natives who had turned away a bit from the economic and cultural
conservatism of their parents. It worked. In 1980—at the height of
the boom—the *Times Herald*, which had started many laps behind,
almost pulled even with the *Morning News* in circulation.

John Bloom was among the brightest of the *Times Herald's* new
crop of bright young reporters. Will Jarrett had remembered him
from a summer Bloom spent as a college intern at the Philadelphia
Inquirer. Jarrett found Bloom in Nashville, where he was editing
a country-club magazine, and hired him, despite the fact that two
other editors who met him thought he was too shy to be a reporter.
Bloom says he was the paper's "fluff specialist" for a while—the reporter papers depend on to write their way out of a story on the
first day of spring or a story on the new baby giraffe at the zoo—
but he also worked on stories about mistreatment of Mexican-

Americans taken into police custody and about a resurgence of the Klan. After only two years on the paper, he was chosen to be what the *Times Herald* called its Texas Ranger—a reporter who roams across the state looking for stories. In 1978, he left to join *Texas Monthly*, a magazine whose young nonfiction writers were bringing it a national reputation, and then, toward the end of 1981, he returned to the *Times Herald* as the movie reviewer. Only a couple of months later, he went to the Century Drive-In in Grand Prairie and discovered Joe Bob Briggs.

There are any number of people on newspapers around the country who could easily be imagined sliding into the character of Joe Bob Briggs—people who wrap themselves in the blue-denim cloak of childhoods in places like west Texas or south Georgia— but John Bloom was not among them. Nothing about him suggested that he might harbor within him a wild nineteen-year-old redneck. Bloom was the son of schoolteachers—Southern Baptists from Texas who, fairly early in his childhood, settled in Little Rock. It was not a childhood spent beating up auto mechanics or watching trashy movies at drive-ins with the likes of May Ellen Masters and Cherry Dilday and the other girls Joe Bob was always describing as "dumb as a box of rocks." As an infant, Bloom had contracted polio, and he spent part of junior high school with a withered right leg in a brace. He grew into a tall, exceedingly thin, almost theatrically handsome young man with pale skin and a thatch of black hair and an almost imperceptible limp. In person, John Bloom would have fulfilled the expectations of a reader who had a strong vision of what a sensitive commentator on the *nouvelle vague* should look like, but he would have been a surprise to readers who had followed the ragged adventures of Joe Bob Briggs. When he is asked why he didn't acknowledge authorship of "Joe Bob Goes to the Drive-In," he sometimes says, "I was almost afraid people would feel disappointed if they met me."

Although Bloom obviously didn't turn out to be too shy to be a reporter, he never really became part of the newsroom crowd. At both the *Times Herald* and *Texas Monthly*, his colleagues thought of him as a sort of outsider, who was likely to have odd hours and odd friends. Editors considered him enormously talented and also quietly intent on having his own way. Partly because Bloom had written long, thoughtful pieces for *Texas Monthly* on an articulate fundamentalist minister and on the Wycliffe Bible Translators, he was sometimes called John the Baptist. People who knew him on *Texas Monthly* tend to use the same phrases when they talk about him, which might suggest a unanimity of opinion except that one of the phrases is "You never really feel you know him." They sometimes spoke of him as Good John and Bad John—the Good John seen as sensitive and intelligent, the Bad John as cold and manipulative—and not many of them felt close enough to him to know which was the actual John Bloom. Neither Good John nor Bad John seemed to presage Joe Bob Briggs. During Bloom's time at *Texas Monthly*, some of his colleagues felt him to be edging toward the right politically but certainly not to the sort of right represented by Joe Bob Briggs, who once wrote that he wasn't terribly happy about being syndicated in San Francisco because "it goes against my principles to write a column for communist-speaking cities." Looking back recently at Bloom's days on *Texas Monthly*, the magazine's editor, Gregory Curtis, said, "I wasn't surprised he could become someone else, but I thought he might have turned into a Baptist preacher."

However unlikely it was, though, John Bloom could, when it came time to write Friday's column, transform himself with great ease into Joe Bob Briggs. Bloom seemed to be among those writers who find the use of an alter ego or a pseudonym liberating: He has said that producing a Joe Bob column took him about three hours, counting the time spent watching the movie. Almost from the beginning, Joe Bob wrote about his own life as well as about such matters as the transvestite wrestling scene in "Chained Heat." Joe Bob might start talking about how he'd asked Junior Stebbens to do a complete overhaul on the Toronado he bought after the demise of the Dodge Dart or about how the young woman he always referred to as Ugly on a Stick "went down to Tex Pawn and tried to get a 30-year breast improvement loan," and almost forget to get around to the movie he had just seen. He always printed let-

ters from readers—preference given to hate mail—and he always
showed no respect in his replies. ("We're talking jerkola at the
minimum. We're probably talking wimp.") Jim Schutze believes
that in those early months Bloom, through local references and
an ear for local language, created not just a generic redneck but
someone representative of the people who had been left out of the
new Dallas—"the people on the fringe of Dallas, this Yankee island,
who were country, who had to drive in for work in their pickups."

Bloom saw Joe Bob not simply as a redneck but as a particularly smart, diabolical, anarchistic redneck who was "full of latent
sexual and violent energies"—someone who wasn't afraid to say
anything. What a country storyteller named Gamble Rogers once
said of the ornery and fearlessly outspoken cracker was a central
feature of Joe Bob's character: "He don't care. He flat do not care."
In fact, Joe Bob took pleasure in saying whatever seemed likely to
offend someone, and his response to finding out that what he said
had indeed given offense was to say it again. (Writing in "Patriotic
Gore" about a Tennessee cracker who was an alter ego of a mid-
nineteenth-century journalist named George Washington Harris,
Edmund Wilson said, "One of the most striking things about *Sut
Lovingood* is that it is all as offensive as possible.") It was a characteristic that made people turn to Joe Bob first thing on Friday
morning—wondering what he might have gone and said now, and
wondering how long he was going to get away with it.

It was also, of course, the characteristic that made the high
sheriffs at the *Times Herald* edgy. Early in Joe Bob's career, they established a special system under which each Joe Bob column was
read by two copy editors, both of whom had instructions to sum-
mon an assistant managing editor at any sign of trouble. It isn't
unusual for Texas writers to use a plainspoken character like Joe
Bob. Molly Ivins, a popular *Times Herald* columnist who's based
in Austin, tends to find her best material in the true adventures
of Texas politicians—the gubernatorial candidate, for instance,
whose fear of AIDS was so strong that on a trip to San Francisco
last spring he wore shower caps on his feet while standing in the
hotel bathtub—but she also refers often to a sort of all-purpose

Texas ol' boy she calls Bubba. Having such a character write the column himself, though, presented some special problems. One of them was what some people called the Archie Bunker factor—the problem of whether the column is making fun of Joe Bob or of the people Joe Bob makes fun of. Also, part of Joe Bob's impact was based on saying something the readers would not have expected him to say. Although Bloom has always denied any strategy beyond trying to make jokes, there was a feeling at the *Times Herald* that Joe Bob had to "up the dosage" every Friday. "John's the sort of guy who wants to push and push," one of the high sheriffs said recently. "Like a college editor trying to get a bad word in the paper." At times, he was precisely like a college editor trying to get a bad word in the paper—the only difference being that the word's excision would provide Joe Bob with a joke about being muzzled by the high sheriffs or by "the jerkola french-fry head communist censors in Washington."

A couple of years after the column began, an editor's note in *Weekend* said that Joe Bob, mentioning such irritations as "too many high sheriffs" and "too many guys named Todd living in Dallas," had left what appeared to be a letter of resignation, written on a page torn from a Big Chief spiral notebook. "Life is a fern bar and I'm out of here," Joe Bob wrote. "I'm history." But Joe Bob was back the next week, praising a movie called "The Being" for an "excellent slime glopola monster with moving mouth." By that time, there were people on the *Times Herald* who thought that the steady increase in dosage would inevitably make Job Bob history sooner or later, and one editor had offered the opinion that the high sheriffs might consider the advantages of simply picking an opportune moment to have Joe Bob's Toronado spin out on the interstate.

It would obviously be unusual under any circumstances for a newspaper to kill its most popular feature. It would have been particularly difficult in the circumstances the *Times Herald* found itself in. By the time the Joe Bob Briggs column had become established, it was clear that the race with the *Morning News* was being lost. There were any number of theories to explain what had happened. The *Morning News*, partly because of the competition and partly from the infusion of some new blood in management, had greatly improved, making up in thoroughness what it might have lacked in sizzle. Its editorial page still might not have given great offense to those who drafted the Dixiecrat platform in 1948, but its news department had, in Will Jarrett's grudging words, "kind of started practicing modern journalism." ("Newspaper competition is usually like high-low poker," Molly Ivins has said. "But in this case both players went high.") Meanwhile, the *Times Herald* was having some problems. For a variety of reasons, it was without strong editorial leadership for a while. There was a newsroom power struggle that sapped a lot of the paper's energy. Some observers outside the paper thought that the management had never learned the prescribed Dallas method of getting along with the business leaders—people who have assumed the synonymy of their interests and the city's interests for so long that they routinely describe any story not respectful to business as "anti-Dallas"—and some reporters inside the paper grumbled that management was beginning to get along with the business leaders too well. Some people thought that the *Times Herald* had, in covering all of those extra laps necessary to catch up with the *Morning News*, simply run out of wind. Among the shrinking bright spots was "Joe Bob Goes to the Drive-In," which might have been the best-read feature in either paper. The *Times Herald* didn't simply tolerate Joe Bob. It put his name on billboards. It sold baseball caps that said, "Joe Bob Briggs Sez Check It Out" and T-shirts that said, "Joe Bob Briggs Is a Close Personal Friend of Mine."

The Baptists had been the first to complain. When it comes to objecting to offenses against public order and morality in Texas, they are rarely beaten to the punch. Southern Baptists are well represented in Dallas—the First Baptist Church, led by the Reverend W. A. Criswell, is the largest Baptist congregation in the entire country—but the first serious complaint from Baptists about Joe Bob Briggs came from a minister in Tyler, who said that Joe Bob's preoccupation with sex and violence revealed a sick mind. The Baptists were not alone. Joe Bob offended gays with some of his San Francisco jokes, and he offended feminists with his Miss Custom Body Contest. Joe Bob offended so many different people that the sheer variety of those he had outraged became part of the standard defense of his column: Joe Bob's admirers said that he was "an equal-opportunity offender." Joe Bob's response to complaints or criticism can be judged from an opinion survey he conducted after a San Francisco film critic named Peter Stack differed with him on whether a movie called "Basket Case" was an inept and disgusting splatter flick or the single best movie of 1982. Inviting the readers to settle the question democratically, Joe Bob provided a ballot that said, "Question: In your opinion, is the french-fry-head San Francisco writer named Peter Stack a wimp or not?" Stack did not come out well in the balloting.

Despite Joe Bob's habit of referring to all females as bimbos and his ubiquitous breast count and his celebration of movies that featured the dismemberment of women ("I'm telling you these bimbos get hacked up until it's chop suey city") and his sponsorship of the Miss Custom Body Contest ("All contestants must be able to count to the number seven, and may not use such a demonstration as their 'talent'"), the first strong attack from feminists didn't come until Joe Bob had been appearing for two years. A lot of women who read the *Times Herald*—including a lot of women who considered themselves feminists—thought Joe Bob was funny. A number of them thought that he served to demonstrate just how ludicrous Texas he-men were. In fact, before it became general knowledge that Joe Bob was a creature of John Bloom, Molly Ivins, who is widely known as a strong feminist, was regularly accused of being the author of "Joe Bob Goes to the Drive-In."

When the attack came, it was led by Charlotte Taft, who runs an abortion clinic called the Routh Street Women's Clinic. At the time, she had been feeling vaguely guilty about not organizing a protest against the local showing of "Pieces," a movie that had been picketed by feminists elsewhere because of its concentration on hideous violence against women. Someone who runs an abortion clinic in Dallas—where right-to-lifers seem to attack in endless waves, like Chinese regulars pouring over the 38th Parallel—

can't always get around to the side issues. Then she came across a capsule review of the movie in the *Times Herald*. The *Weekend* section had got into the habit of running capsules by both of its movie reviewers, distinguishing them only by the initials at the end. Between reviews by JB of "The Osterman Weekend" (one star) and "The Right Stuff" (a star and a half), JBB's capsule review of "Pieces" said, "Best chainsaw flick since the original 'Saw,' about a gonzo geek pervert who goes around a college campus cutting up coeds into itty bitty pieces. Two heads roll. Arms roll. Legs roll. Something else rolls. Nine living breasts, two dead breasts. No motor vehicle chases. Gratuitous kung fu. Eight corpses. One beast with a chainsaw. Four gallons of blood. Not much talking. Splatter City. Joe Bob says check it out." The review included Joe Bob's rating: four stars.

Casting around for allies, Charlotte Taft found support from an old adversary—William Murchison, a conservative columnist on the *Morning News*. Murchison wrote that the celebration of a movie like "Pieces" was not simply a feminist issue but a humanity issue—a reminder that people who make movies seem to take no notice of someone like Mother Teresa but think nothing of turning out a movie that "devalues the human species." The reply in Joe Bob's column was headlined "JOE BOB ATTACKED BY COMMUNIST FRIEND OF MOTHER TERESA." In it Joe Bob said, "Last week this royal jerkola with a bad haircut named William Murchison wrote a column called 'Chain-Sawing Our Culture.' He wrote it on the *editorial* page of the Dallas Morning Snooze. . . . It has this itty bitty picture of Willie Murchison with his lips mashed together like the zombie-monster in 'Dr. Tarr's Torture Garden,' and his eyes look exactly like the guy in 'I Drink Your Blood.' He also has a little resemblance to the woman-carver in 'I Dismember Mama,' but I'm sure that's just a coincidence." A couple of weeks later, Joe Bob finally got down to the issues at hand: "*Numero uno:* I have enormous respect for women. Especially when they have garbanzas the size of Cleveland. *Numero two-o:* I am violently opposed to the use of chainsaws, power drills, tire tools, rubber hoses, brass knuckles, bob wire, hypodermics, embalming needles or poleaxes against women, unless it is *necessary* to the plot. *Numero three-o:* I don't believe in slapping women around, unless they want it. *Numero four-o:* I would like to settle this matter in the easiest way possible, so I hereby challenge Charlotte Taft to a nude mud-wrestling match. . . ."

Charlotte Taft decided that a better way to settle it was to organize a letter-writing campaign to the *Times Herald*. It was based on the same argument she had made in her letter to the editor—that men in Dallas still seemed to think it was all right to make jokes about violence against women, decades after a supposedly responsible newspaper would dare find anything funny about, say, ridiculing black people. Eventually, though, the feminists decided that their efforts were going nowhere. The editors of the *Times Herald* seemed uninterested. The feminists themselves were by no means unanimous in condemning Joe Bob. Molly Ivins, for one, said that the complaints were "displaced anger." Interviewed for a feature on Joe Bob by KERA, the local public-television station, she said that what should be protested was "the vicious and degrading pornography" of exploitation movies, not someone who was "making brilliant fun of the kind of people who go to watch those movies." Charlotte Taft was never won over to that point of view. "John Bloom wanted to have it both ways—some readers taking it at face value and some taking it as satire," she said not long ago. "But part of satire is to instruct, not to wallow in the fun of saying what's not supposed to be said. If there's an Archie Bunker, there has to be a Meathead. What I saw in it was self-indulgence—the self-indulgence of someone who wants to tell a racist joke and pretends to be making fun of someone telling a racist joke. It was indulging in an adult the humor of a seventh-grader—a seventh-grade boy." She had decided, though, that all she was doing in her protest was providing material for Joe Bob, who wrote a lot about the high sheriffs' being pressured by what he always referred to as the National Organization for Bimbos.

John Bloom agreed that protest was just playing into Joe Bob's hands. On the KERA program, he was interviewed as Joe Bob's closest friend, and he said of the attacks by feminists, "One thing

Joe Bob's critics should learn is that you should never attack an anarchist. He has nothing to lose." Using criticism as material for making fun of the critic was among the characteristics that, after two years, had been established firmly enough to be an unvarying part of Joe Bob's character. He could be counted on to reoffend the offended, just as he could be counted on to refer to women as bimbos, and to persist in trying to sneak in words that the high sheriffs considered inappropriate. John Bloom and Ron Smith and the other people at the *Times Herald* who dealt with Joe Bob, all of whom spoke of him in the third person even among themselves, still had the power to arrange for his Toronado to spin out on the interstate, of course. But as long as Joe Bob existed he was, in certain ways, on his own.

H e's *gone* to all these movies," Charlotte Taft has said. "I find that kind of scary." Even those who didn't find it eerie that an honors graduate of Vanderbilt could thrive on a steady diet of splatter flicks might have wondered just how many chain-saw dismemberments and kung-fu battles anyone could sit through without becoming too bored even to maintain an accurate body count. As it turned out, though, John Bloom got tired of movie-reviewing before Joe Bob did. In 1984, Bloom gave up reviewing to become the paper's Metro columnist—someone responsible for three columns a week. Writing the Metro column was considered a full-time job, but once a week Bloom continued to turn into Joe Bob Briggs. In January of 1985, that became twice a week. Blackie Sherrod, one of the most popular sportswriters in Dallas, had jumped to the *Morning News,* and the *Times Herald* countered with a new sports-writer of its own—Joe Bob Briggs. Bloom had actually started out in newspapers writing sports for the Arkansas *Democrat* while he was still in high school; he went through Vanderbilt on a Grantland Rice Scholarship, awarded by the Thoroughbred Racing Associations. Will Jarrett has said that he saw the sports column, "Jock Talk with Joe Bob," as more than simply a counter to Sherrod. "I thought of it as Phase Two," he said not long ago. "The bimbo thing was kind of played out. He was depending a lot on ethnic humor. There was a lot of material in sports. John knew the field. It was a way to ride his popularity and get rid of some of the problem areas." Even writing about sports, of course, Joe Bob did not avoid the problem areas completely. In one of the first "Jock Talk" columns, he managed to make up a Boston Celtics theme song called "Attack of the Stupid White People" and to refer to Tony Nathan, of the Miami Dolphins, as "the only slow Negro in the NFL."

Will Jarrett had been off editing the Denver *Post* during most of the time Joe Bob was steadily dismantling many of the barriers against tastelessness the high sheriffs had erected, and he says that when he returned to Dallas, in 1984, he was surprised to see what Joe Bob was getting away with. There were occasional flareups from offended readers—there were complaints from members of Mothers Against Drunk Driving (MADD), for instance, when Joe Bob organized a group called Drunks Against Mad Mothers (DAMM)—but Jarrett got the impression that a lot of readers had been following Joe Bob Briggs long enough to shrug off most of what he said as just the sort of thing Joe Bob would say. *Times Herald* editors had never truly lost their nervousness about running the column, though, and some people around the newsroom were, in fact, troubled by what they saw as an increasing reliance on ethnic cracks. Reviewing a movie called "Breakin'," for instance, Joe Bob managed to mention not simply "Negro Dancing" but also "Meskins," the perils he saw in Vietnamese immigration ("Pretty soon you can't go in 7-Eleven without wondering whether those guys are putting dog meat in the frozen burritos"), and a character "whose idea of a good time is to go sit on the beach with guys from the chorus line and talk about their Liberace record collections, if you know what I mean and I think you do"—all in the course of saying that he had been shown the path from racism by his friend Bobo Rodriguez: "I never did ask Bobo what race he was, but I'm pretty sure he was a Negro. His skin was the color of Taster's Choice Decaffeinated, which means he could go either way, but one time he tried to change his name to Bobo al-Salaam, and when he did that everybody started calling him 'Al' because they thought he was saying 'Al Sloan.'"

Although some of Joe Bob's fans around the *Times Herald* may have fallen away, he was publicly more popular than ever. His column was being syndicated to fifty papers or so, making him a figure of renown even in San Francisco—a place he normally referred to as "Wimp Capital of the World" or "Geek City, U.S.A." He was so popular in Cleveland that when the editors of the *Plain Dealer* decided to drop his column for tastelessness an avalanche of reader mail persuaded them to put it back. In some film circles, he was a sort of cult figure—someone who could attract Stephen King to the Third Annual World Drive-In Movie Festival and Custom Car Rally. There were those, though, who thought that Joe Bob's national popularity was his undoing. They thought that "the golden age of Joe Bob" had been in the early months of the column, when Joe Bob could be understood in a local context and could spice up his column with local stunts, like organizing a letter-writing campaign to the public official he held responsible for the removal of the drive-in-movie screens at Texas Stadium ("Dear French-fry Head Mayor of Irving . . ."). There were those who thought Joe Bob's undoing was that Bloom was spreading himself too thin by writing five columns a week. Theories about Joe Bob's undoing were widely discussed and closely analyzed in the spring of 1985, because on one April Friday the worst fears that *Times Herald* high sheriffs had entertained about the Joe Bob Briggs column finally materialized.

The offending column, published a couple of months after rock stars gathered in California to record a song for African famine relief, was headlined "JOE BOB, DRIVE-IN ARTISTS JOIN FORCES FOR MINORITIES WITH 'WE ARE THE WEIRD.'" Joe Bob said that the best-known drive-in artists in the world had gathered together to sing the song: "They all stood there, swaying from side to side, arms linked (except for The Mutant, who don't have arms) and singing their little hearts out." Although Joe Bob's song does not lend itself to summary—it's never precisely clear who's singing about exactly what—the first chorus was representative of its tone:

> We are the weird.
> We are the starvin,
> We are the scum of the filthy earth,
> So let's start scarfin...
> There's a goat-head bakin
> We're calling it their food,
> If the Meskins can eat it,
> They can eat it, too.

The drive-in stars' recording was, Joe Bob wrote, "for the benefit of minority groups in Africa and the United Negro College Fund in the United States, cause I think we should be sending as many Negroes to college as we can, specially the stupid Negroes."

It wasn't immediately clear how such a column found its way into the *Times Herald* and the distribution network of the Los Angeles Times Syndicate. The copy editors apparently had not flagged an assistant managing editor. According to one rather ornate theory, Joe Bob had for months been trying to sneak the word "twat" past the two copy editors, and they were concentrating so hard on spotting it—examining each syllable in the name of any town Joe Bob invented, searching any new organization for contraband acronyms—that they weren't paying enough attention to the content of the column. According to another theory, the copy editors, after a few years of reading Joe Bobbian copy, had grown desensitized, as some people are said to get after prolonged exposure to pornography. Bloom has always insisted that a managing editor who happened to walk by his desk and glance at the column on his computer monitor read the entire song, laughed, and said, "Great stuff!"

There were plenty of readers around Dallas who were as accustomed to Joe Bob's ways as the copy editors were, but not many of these readers were black. Even though the black community regarded the *Times Herald* as the newspaper sympathetic to its interests, "Joe Bob Goes to the Drive-In" had never attracted a wide black readership. The first Joe Bob column that a lot of black people in Dallas read was the column that included a famine-relief song with verses like:

> Send em a heart so they'll know that someone cares
> And a lung, and an elbow, and three big toes.
> As the Big Guy told us, we should always clean our plate,
> Cause then all the Africans' stomachs won't look gross.

"After a while, you get sort of used to Joe Bob," Ron Smith has said. "But if you read that thing flat cold it'll send chills up your spine. And that's the way a lot of black people read it."

Willis Johnson, who runs a morning talk show on KKDA, Dallas's leading black radio station, was not in the habit of reading Joe Bob's column, but he got a call from a listener—a reporter for the *Morning News*, as it happened—who told him he would do well to make an exception in this case. Johnson, who was outraged by the column, read it over the air, and the mounting rage soon monopolized his program. The *Times Herald* was also having serious trouble within its own building. Black *Times Herald* employees from a number of departments were furious about the column, and a meeting at which Bloom tried to explain himself only made things worse. By then, it was obvious that the outrage over the "We Are the Weird" column was of another order than the customary Joe Bob controversies that always blew over after some angry letters and a few Joe Bobbian jokes at the complainants' expense. One of Willis Johnson's callers had been John Wiley Price, a black county commissioner. Price is among a small group of militant black officeholders in Dallas who have tried to ease aside the black ministers whose style of leadership flowed from the old accommodation with the white business community. On the air, Price and Johnson agreed to go downtown on Tuesday afternoon, right after a weekly black-leadership lunch, and demand to know why the *Times Herald*, the newspaper that supposedly represented fair treatment for minorities in Dallas, had on its staff someone who used phrases like "stupid Negroes" and found it humorous to ridicule starving people in Africa. When they arrived that Tuesday afternoon, they found that they had been joined by several hundred other people. In a city that had basically skipped the public confrontations of the civil-rights struggle, the presence of a large crowd of black people marching into a white institution in an angry mood was virtually unprecedented.

Jarrett and two other editors met with as many of the protesters as could be jammed into a small auditorium. The room was hot, and got even hotter when television lights were turned on. The people in the audience were fanning themselves with whatever was at hand. The three editors, surrounded by protesters, were sweating. That morning's edition had already printed an apology of a completeness that Will Jarrett called unique in his years of newspaper experience: "Joe Bob Briggs' column that appeared in Friday's *Times Herald* offended many readers. The *Times Herald* deeply regrets that the column was published. It was a misdirected attempt at satire. A great deal of insensitivity was reflected in the column. We apologize." But the crowd did not seem satisfied with an apology, however abject. "One apology in one postage-stamp-size corner of the front page is not enough," a black attorney said. "This column needs to be gone." Jarrett started out by saying that the question of whether "Joe Bob Goes to the Drive-In" would be run in the next Friday's paper was still being considered, but after a number of angry speeches he finally said, "I'm deeply concerned about it. I'm deeply concerned about the reaction. I'm deeply concerned about the staff reaction to it. So the Joe Bob Briggs column, the *Weekend* column, the drive-in-movie column, is dead." In a much smaller, more conventional meeting a few days later, the *Times Herald* pledged that twelve of the next twenty-two editorial positions filled would be filled by members of a minority. But for most of the black people of Dallas nothing could quite match the exhilaration of that public capitulation in the steamy auditorium, right there in front of the television cameras. Above the cheers that followed Jarrett's announcement the voice of a woman in the

first few rows could be heard shouting, in triumph and amazement, "We did it! We did it!"

J ohn Bloom was a hundred and fifty miles away from Dallas
that afternoon, delivering a speech at Texas A&M. Will Jarrett drove out to Dallas–Fort Worth Airport to meet Bloom's return flight, but the plane had arrived early; Bloom was already on
his way back to the city. It was days before they finally met again.
Bloom wouldn't talk to Jarrett on the telephone. He was hurt and
angry. He saw the front-page apology as a writer being "publicly
disavowed by his own newspaper, not for any factual error or mis-
representation, but purely because his opinion is unpopular." He
considered the way that Jarrett had cancelled the column—publicly, without telling the columnist—basically unforgivable. Jarrett, who had brought Bloom to Dallas and remained close to him
in the years that followed, was astonished that Bloom wouldn't
come to the phone. "What I was worried about was John Bloom,"
he has said. "I realized that Joe Bob was more important to him
than John Bloom was. John Bloom wouldn't talk to his editor for
three days, even though Joe Bob had done the damage. I didn't fire
John Bloom. I fired a mythical character John Bloom had always
said he didn't agree with. Why was he mad at me?"

Jarrett had hoped that Bloom would continue writing his own
column, and maybe even the "Jock Talk with Joe Bob" column. But
John Bloom decided to resign from the *Times Herald*. In a final
Metro column, which Jarrett declined to print, Bloom wrote that
the real issue was not racism but the fact that some subjects, like
African famine relief, had been put off limits for satire because
"they are too close to our subconscious fears and guilts," and he
reminded Jarrett of the newsroom sign that had said, "THE ONLY
SACRED COW HERE IS HAMBURGER." He didn't discuss the
offending column except to say that on the question of who the
"we" was in lines like "we are the scum of the filthy earth"—the
question that some *Times Herald* people referred to as Joe Bob's
pronoun problem—"I realize I'm the person who should know the
answer to this question, but I'm afraid I was too busy laughing to

worry about Joe Bob's illogic." By the time Bloom resigned, there couldn't have been many people left in Dallas who were still unaware of the true authorship of the "Joe Bob Goes to the Drive-In" column—all pretense had been dropped in the barrage of news coverage of the controversy—but Bloom said he was resigning in sympathy with Joe Bob.

No one else at the *Times Herald* showed much sympathy. A lot of *Times Herald* reporters—and a lot of other Dallas reporters—were indeed horrified at what seemed to be a capitulation under pressure in the *Times Herald* auditorium. "It created a precedent that's dangerous," Molly Ivins has said. "I know that Reverend Criswell could have five thousand people there about me at the drop of a hat." But that didn't translate into newsroom support for Joe Bob. In fact, most of the people in the newsroom had, in the first days of the controversy, signed a bulletin-board statement demanding that Joe Bob's column be more closely edited in the future. *Times Herald* reporters did not see what had happened as a case of one of their own being crushed by management. They didn't consider John Bloom one of their own. Not many of them actually knew him, and some of them may have resented him with the special resentment reporters reserve for someone who seems to be getting away with the sort of writing that would be routinely edited out of their own copy. Some of them, particularly the younger ones, had long felt that it was dishonest for a newspaper to keep up the pretense that a fictional columnist actually existed. Also, as Jim Schutze put it recently, "they were the ones who answered the phone when people started calling in and saying, 'The trouble is these colored people don't know good say-tire when they see it.'"

Even more important, a lot of the reporters simply hated the "We Are The Weird" column. They didn't know who the "we" in the song was, either—figuring out how the humor worked in the column required an almost scholarly knowledge of Joe Bobbian context—but, unlike Bloom, they weren't too busy laughing to care. Satire is obviously most offensive when the reader's first response isn't laughter; it lies there, waiting to be analyzed. Those in the newsroom who thought Joe Bob's problem was more in his delivery than in his subject matter pointed out that the rock stars' African-relief effort was not, in fact, a sacred cow; a number of political cartoonists and columnists had already taken a crack at it. But the column's subject matter was at the heart of the opposition. "Satire is a weapon you use against the powerful," Molly Ivins, who was not on Joe Bob's side this time, has said. "You don't use satire against the weak." Bloom's position seemed to be that a truly liberal society wouldn't recognize any subject as off limits: now that black people are equal partners in modern, postsegregationist America, it would be patronizing not to subject them equally to the occasional satiric knock. What people like Molly Ivins found wrong with that was the assumption that black people are now equal partners in modern America. Presumably, most people at the *Times Herald* would have agreed with Bloom that these days a newspaper columnist is a lot less likely to get away with a joke about starving Africans or "stupid Negroes" than with a joke about the President, but not many of them seemed to think it followed that such jokes had to be made.

"For forty-eight hours, I thought, Well, it's over. It's gone up in flames. And it's kind of an ignominious end," Bloom said not long ago. "Then I started getting these letters. A large number of responsible editors and reporters had been saying, 'The guy got what he deserved,' but the readers were saying, 'You can't let them do this.' Joe Bob was always responsive to readers." The column had been dropped by the Los Angeles Times Syndicate as well as by the *Times Herald*, but, without missing a week, Joe Bob signed with the Universal Press Syndicate, which has some experience with controversy as the distributors of Garry Trudeau's "Doonesbury." The first Universal column dealt, of course, with the *Times Herald* decision to kill the column—or with the assassination of Joe Bob in Dallas, as Bloom saw it.

"November 22, 1963. April 16, 1985," the column began. "They said it couldn't happen again.

"I guess I'll always remember where I was when they killed me on national TV, right after the Maybelline commercial. I guess we all will. Who couldn't remember the look on the High Sheriff's face when he said, 'Joe Bob's dead!' . . . Even though the High Sheriff was arrested at the scene by TV reporters with bad hair, there were immediate rumors of an international communist conspiracy, the 'three-gun theory,' the 'act of God theory,' the bizarre 'one-garbanza theory,' and the 'What would happen if you dropped Joe Bob Briggs off a seven-story building and watched him splatter all over the pavement?' theory." After some Joe Bobbian talk about the protest and a list of astonishing coincidences ("Lincoln and Kennedy were both assassinated on a Friday. Joe Bob was assassinated on a Tuesday. Makes you think"), Joe Bob found space for a quick summary of a movie called "Lust in the Dust": "Four breasts. Fifteen dead bodies. One riot. One brawl. One gang rape, with midget. Two quarts blood. One beast (Divine). Thigh crushing. Bullwhip fu. Nekkid bimbo-wrestling . . ." It would have been uncharacteristic, of course, for Joe Bob to acknowledge any regrets about the "We Are the Weird" column or apologize to those it might have offended, and Bloom, when asked about an apology, tends to say something like "Apologize for what? There's not a single fact in the column. They say it's insensitive and in poor taste. Well, Joe Bob is insensitive and in poor taste. I'll admit that."

The decision of the *Times Herald* to kill the Joe Bob drive-in column, which John Bloom seems to have heard as a decision to kill Joe Bob, served to make Joe Bob a much larger part of John Bloom's life. Bloom continued to write under his own name—eventually, he began doing a monthly piece for Dallas's city magazine, *D*, and he started a book on Route 66—but in the freelance market Joe Bob Briggs was likely to get more assignments than John Bloom. For one thing, he was much better known, particularly after the "We Are the Weird" controversy. John Bloom is one of a number of talented young Texas writers. Joe Bob Briggs is a writer who can provide a unique way for *Film Comment* to deal with exploitation movies or for *Rolling Stone* to deal with the end of the Texas boom. Writing under his own name, Bloom had difficulty finding a publisher for a serious nonfiction book he and another *Texas Monthly* writer, Jim Atkinson, wrote about a Texas murder;

it was finally published by the Texas Monthly Press. As Joe Bob Briggs, he had assumed, correctly, that there were big-shot publishers in New York interested in getting filthy rich off his books.

The change was more than Joe Bob's simply easing out of the three-hour-a-week compartment Bloom had kept him in. A couple of months after Bloom left the *Times Herald*, his agent got a call from someone in Cleveland who offered to set up a speaking engagement for Joe Bob Briggs. Bloom, who had not even officially admitted writing the Joe Bob column until the "We Are the Weird" controversy erupted, decided to accept the date as Joe Bob. In a high school just outside Cleveland, he did a sort of one-man show, costumed in a cowboy hat and a more pronounced drawl. After that, those who phoned Bloom's agent with lecture inquiries were asked whether they were interested in John Bloom or Joe Bob Briggs. Joe Bob's rates were higher.

Bloom has said that in those first months of being on his own he was intent on keeping Joe Bob alive, partly because he was convinced that the high sheriffs' intentions toward Joe Bob continued to be murderous. Their weapon was a copyright. Although no objection had been raised to the Universal Press Syndicate's distribution of "Joe Bob Goes to the Drive-In," the *Times Herald* warned Dell, which was about to publish a collection of Joe Bobbiana, that John Bloom owned neither the name Joe Bob Briggs nor the rights to the material that had appeared in the *Times Herald*. The argument over rights exacerbated a hostility that already carried the special bitterness of a disagreement between people who had once been close. In his stage appearances as Joe Bob, Bloom had taken to referring to his old employer as the *Slimes Herald* and singing a song about how he'd like to make "editor fondue" out of the high sheriff who fired him—a high sheriff who happened to be John Bloom's old friend and mentor, Will Jarrett. ("A heart attack would do it, or trampled by a mob, or eaten by a giant bumblebee.")

Bloom claimed that the paper wanted to prevent the publication of Joe Bob's books out of spite. The high sheriffs of the *Times Herald* and the Times Mirror Company were indeed furious about

the "We Are the Weird" incident—some of them saw it as one hor-
rifying column destroying a position with the minority community that had taken years to establish—and they were apparently
wounded by Joe Bob's insults. At one point, the paper offered to
release the material under conditions that included a promise not
to ridicule the *Times Herald* or its executives. The proposed agreement would also have given the paper control over which columns appeared in a book. Jarrett has said that the main issue was
whether the *Times Herald* could acquiesce in the republication of
the "We Are the Weird" column: "We'd be in the position of saying,
'Right, this is awful, it should never have been printed, we're going to kill the column,' and then turning around and saying, 'Sure,
go ahead and publish it in a book, make a lot of money.' The black
people would have said we were hypocrites." Bloom rejected the
proposed agreement, and after months of meetings and lawyers'
letters and phone calls he filed legal papers against the *Times Herald* in an attempt to liberate Joe Bob Briggs.

L ast summer, a little more than a year after the cancellation
of the column, Bloom's lawyer won a declaratory judgment
on one of the two questions at issue—the question of who had a
right to use the name Joe Bob Briggs—and a date was set to hear
arguments on whether Bloom had the right to reprint the columns
that had appeared in the *Times Herald*. Outside the courtroom,
the blood-feud aspect of the disagreement had begun to dissipate.
Will Jarrett had already left the paper, in a purge that also claimed
some executives on the business side. Not long after the declaratory judgment, the Times Mirror Company, in what the New York
Times story called "an apparent acknowledgment that it was unable to win the heated Dallas newspaper war," announced that it
was selling the *Times Herald*. The buyer was a young, Texas-born
newspaper magnate who said he was moving the headquarters of
his enterprises from New Jersey to Dallas and intended to become
active in "the Dallas leadership community." The Joe Bob suit was
specifically excluded from the assets and liabilities passed on to
the new owner, and it was assumed that the sale had completed

the transformation of the Joe Bob controversy from a serious al-
tercation into the sort of loose end that a large corporation likes to
have tied up before it leaves town. Times Mirror and John Bloom
quickly settled their differences, and Dell made plans to publish
the collection in the form Bloom wanted it published. Joe Bob, in
effect, belonged to John Bloom.

A lot of Bloom's old colleagues do not think he won a great as-
set. "What bothers me is that John Bloom is a significant talent
who can endure, and Joe Bob is an ephemeral kind of thing," one
of them said recently. "If John thinks no one else can kill Joe Bob,
fine. Then at some point he should kill Joe Bob himself." The syndicated Joe Bob column is in fact a marginal operation. It appears
in a few dozen newspapers, but a lot of them are college papers
or alternative weeklies. The pattern, Bloom says, is that the feature editor buys the column, it runs once, and the executive editor
cancels it. It's a difficult column to sell. The reason is partly the
traditional cautiousness of newspapers—Bloom has always maintained that the only reason Joe Bob appears outrageous is that the
material surrounding him is so bland—but it is also partly that the
"We Are the Weird" controversy gave Joe Bob a reputation not
simply for controversy but also for racism.

Joe Bob's one-man show has been polished considerably since
its rather shaky start in Cleveland. He has even put out a video,
called "Joe Bob Briggs Dead in Concert." Like a lot of shy people
who have to transform themselves into public characters, Bloom
uses hats in the stage show—a cowboy hat, a feed hat, one of those
caps that have horns extending from the sides. Joe Bob tells stories about bimbos and Baptists and a county where the major industry is dirt. He sings songs like "Dirt Mine Blues" and "We Are
the Weird" (with the words significantly toned down). This fall, he
used his column to recruit a troupe of seriously overweight young
women, and in a Dallas appearance on the weekend of the Texas-
Oklahoma game he worked them into the act as the Dancing Bo-
vina Sisters, doing dances like the Frito Stomp. People who know
John Bloom tend to be surprised that he's as fluid as he is onstage,
but the act has received mixed reviews. One of the problems of

Joe Bob's coming to life was pointed out a couple of years ago by Bloom himself, when he was explaining to Dennis Holder, in the *Washington Journalism Review*, why Joe Bob could never be on television: "This thing is so fragile that the last thing you'd want is to remove the mystery and magic through the cold reality of a camera. If you ever gave Joe Bob a specific face, or even a voice, some of the power would be lost." Onstage, Bloom plays a redneck who tells stories, but that may disappoint people who hope to see the real Joe Bob. A headline in the San Francisco *Chronicle* after Joe Bob's appearance in the Wimp Capital of the World said "JOE BOB 'LIVE' IS A PUSSYCAT." Molly Ivins says that even without having seen the act she knows that Bloom can't be very persuasive as Joe Bob Briggs. "For one thing, he's too good-looking," she said not long ago. "If he could act, he'd play the young Byron."

"I'm bothered that he's given up serious journalism for a cardboard cowboy," Will Jarrett said recently. In general, Bloom's former colleagues tend to talk about him the way a bunch of medievalists would talk about one of their number who had gone off to write potboilers. Their theories of just why Bloom is hanging on so hard to Joe Bob depend a bit on what they thought of him in the first place. Some people think it's just pure stubbornness. Some think that under Bloom's shy exterior was always a lust for show business; they point out that he became pals with some Hollywood types during his regular movie-reviewing days, and that he has appeared in a scene (later cut) in the sequel to "Texas Chainsaw Massacre." Some people think that Bloom sees Joe Bob as a ticket to fame and fortune, and some people think that Bloom sat through so many splatter movies "his brain got fried." Some people think that John Bloom, no matter how enlightened and how educated, simply had a wild, racist redneck inside him, and that the redneck has finally surfaced; they tend to say, "John Bloom has become Joe Bob Briggs." Bloom himself says that he'll kill off Joe Bob when he gets tired of him. "Maybe I'll do it until I find the heart of Joe Bob, find out what about him disturbs people," he said recently. "When you see what a threat Joe Bob is to people, the issue becomes the integrity of Joe Bob."

Joe Bob Briggs is no longer much of a presence in Dallas. His column appears in a weekly paper, *The Observer*, and there are still plenty of hard-core Joe Bob fans. But the day is past when all Friday-morning talk seemed to center on what Joe Bob had gone and said now. These days, on Friday morning or any other morning, the talk in Dallas's shiny new office buildings is likely to be about how many square feet of the building remain unleased; the people driving into the city in pickups are likely to be concerned about whether a job will still be there when they arrive. When Joe Bob's mentioned, it's often in the past tense. "The trouble with the character was that he had to push it further and further," Molly Ivins said not long ago. "The poor bastard just outlived his time." The talk about how Joe Bob's column ended sounds a bit like the talk that could be heard in some other American cities twenty years ago—some white people saying that militant blacks were simply looking for an issue, and militant blacks saying that *of course* they were looking for an issue. For a while, people like Willis Johnson thought that the success in galvanizing people around the issue of Joe Bob Briggs might awaken what was sometimes referred to as the sleeping giant of the Dallas black community. They thought that the victory in the *Times Herald* auditorium might serve as an impetus for a more confrontational approach in dealing with the white business community. But there is now a widespread feeling that the giant stretched and then went back to sleep. Johnson says that he and John Wiley Price have been subjected to some criticism among the traditional leadership for not trying to settle differences with the *Times Herald* in a quieter way. Charlotte Taft is still at the Routh Street Women's Clinic. One set of fundamentalists shows up to picket on Wednesday, another set pickets on Saturday, and the Catholics have set up next door in one of those operations whose advertising and name seem designed to attract young women who think they're going to an abortion clinic but find themselves in a place dedicated to talking them out of it. Sometimes, Charlotte Taft gets discouraged. When she ponders the difficulty of financing her operation through the usual fundraising events, she said with a smile not long ago, she sometimes thinks she might have been too quick in rejecting Joe Bob's nude-mud-wrestling challenge.

The *Times Herald* now has the same problem every other daily newspaper has in figuring out how to cover trashy movies. The paper is under new management, and there has been a lot of turnover in staff. Some people on and off the paper say that the controversy over Joe Bob was what finally pushed the Times Mirror Company into giving up on the Dallas newspaper war. There were, of course, solid business reasons for selling the *Times Herald*, which had just dipped into the red after fifteen years of considerable profits. The Dallas boom had fizzled. The war with the *Morning News* had been lost. The resources of the Times Mirror Company could presumably be better invested elsewhere. Those who say that the Joe Bob episode was the last straw for Times Mirror—the experience that soured it forever on Dallas—seem to mean that more symbolically or spiritually than literally. In the words of Ron Smith, one of the people who brought Joe Bob into the world, dealing with the "We Are the Weird" controversy was for the Times Mirror Company "like biting into a bad clam."

The advertising campaign of the new management features a picture of the new editor saying, "Nobody wants to read a wimp newspaper." It is said that the use of a Joe Bobbian word is a coincidence, but there is a temptation to see some connection between the strong anti-wimp statement and the fact that the capitulation in the auditorium left some lingering taint of wimpiness in the building. It also left a new verb in Dallas– "to Joe Bob," meaning to march on an institution with an intimidating number of citizens and hope to buffalo that institution into changing some policy. When Jim Schutze wrote a column critical of one of the black ministers in Dallas some time ago, for instance, the response of one of the minister's supporters was the threat "We're going to come down there and Joe Bob your ass." Some people on the *Times Herald* resent the part played by both John Bloom and management in creating the situation that led to the verb's existence, and some of the same people miss the excitement of those Friday mornings when everyone turned to *Weekend* to see who had been called a

Communist French-fry head this week. Talking about the career of Joe Bob Briggs at the Dallas *Times Herald* recently, Ron Smith said that Shelby Coffey III, who was the editor of the paper at the time the Times Mirror Company sold it, once turned down an idea for a satirical feature by remarking, "This paper has a sorry history on satire"—an allusion, of course, to Joe Bob Briggs. "I took exception to that," Smith said. "I don't think it was sorry. I think it was a noble experiment that went awry."

—1986

ONE TEXAN IN EIGHT LINES

"We have sort of become a nation of whiners..."
 —Phil Gramm in the *Washington Times*

As Senator, Phil was among the designers
Of laws that helped Enron, which showed no decliners,
Manipulate prices of oil from refiners.
(Its stock can be used in your cat box, for liners.)
His laws helped the mortgage thieves rook naïve signers,
Who then lost their houses and can't afford diners.
So now he decides we're a nation of whiners.
Figures.

—2008

REFORMER

It is customary for any woman in politics who is against the established regime to be called feisty, more or less the way any elderly black sharecropper whose picture is taken by a magazine photographer is spoken of as having great dignity. Frances (Sissy) Farenthold, a state legislator from Corpus Christi who just lost a runoff for the Democratic gubernatorial nomination in Texas, was occasionally called feisty during the campaign by some visiting reporter, but the *Texas Observer*—a liberal Austin biweekly that happens to have as its principal editors two women who are sometimes called feisty themselves—titled its cover story on her last year "A Melancholy Rebel." When Mrs. Farenthold said during the campaign that a "private government" of special interests controls the state capitol, she seemed to be expressing disappointment even more than anger. Her voice often had a tone of weary resignation, as if nothing would please her more than to hear that everyone in Austin had reformed and thus relieved her of the unpleasant duty of dealing once more with a tiresome subject. When asked about her mood by reporters, Mrs. Farenthold sometimes said it derived partly from her experiences during the two years she served as director of a legal-services program in her home county, just before her election to the Texas House of Representatives. An alternate theory is that anybody who has seriously worked for change through three sessions of the Texas House of Representatives is fortunate to escape with a melancholy frame of mind instead of severe, disabling depression.

Mrs. Farenthold went to Austin in 1968 with the idea of working for welfare reform—having come to the conclusion that the welfare laws had a lot to do with the pathetic condition of her clients in Nueces County—but she eventually became identified with reform of the state government itself. The Sharpstown stock-fraud scandal—a complicated series of events tied together by the passage of some banking legislation and the stock profits of some people who were helpful in passing it—made corruption the most important issue in Texas politics during her second term in the House. Normally, officeholders in a state like Texas have differed from eminent public servants in the federal government primarily in the way some social scientists claim that lower-class Americans differ from those Americans who have arrived at the middle class—an inability to defer reward. A commissioner of an important federal regulatory agency is content to live on his government salary, secure in the knowledge that his next job may be as a highly paid executive or counsel in the industry he has been regulating. Distinguished Washington lawyers who serve as deputy secretaries of one department or another are ordinarily not given large retainers to use their influence until after they resign their posts. In some states, though, it is understood that such patience is too much to ask of a poor frail human being who happens to find himself governor. In Texas, participatory democracy has meant that leading Democrats can participate in the most lucrative business deals. During her campaign for governor, Mrs. Farenthold would sometimes ask her audience, "How long has it been since we've had a governor who left office without a ranch?" When Orval Faubus left the governorship of Arkansas, he was asked how he had managed to build a two-hundred-thousand-dollar house after having earned only ten thousand dollars a year during his twelve years in office, and he said he owed it all to thrift.

What brought Sissy Farenthold to prominence was that the Sharpstown scandal was blatant enough to offend the voters but not the Legislature. In the House, Mrs. Farenthold's resolution calling for an independent committee to investigate the scandal drew the support of only thirty out of a hundred and fifty members—a group that became known in Austin as the Dirty Thirty. But it soon became obvious that even Texans who are relatively tolerant about how the temptations of high public office might strain a man's patience were shocked by the Sharpstown disclosures. Voters never seem shocked at hearing about the impersonal forces that actually control a state government. Nobody seemed surprised during the campaign, for instance, at Mrs. Farenthold's disclosure that there were a hundred and seventeen utility lobbyists registered at the last session of the Texas Legislature and that Texas remains one of the few states in the country without statewide regulation of utility rates. Candidates for governorships around the country rarely bother to bring up the fact that the state regulatory agencies that do exist are often controlled by the industry they are supposedly regulating. (When Mississippi's insurance commission authorized a rate increase after Hurricane Camille, the commission consisted of two insurance agents and a lawyer for insurance companies.) But personal corruption can make voters angry. In Texas, there has been much more interest in how relatives of some legislators managed to end up on the payroll of other legislators than in how Texas manages to remain one of the four states in the union without a corporate income tax.

When the governor of Texas, Preston Smith, who profited personally in some stock transactions connected with the Sharpstown case, decided to run for renomination in the Democratic primary this spring anyway, he was given little chance of success. Dolph Briscoe, a millionaire banker and rancher from Uvalde, who had finished fourth after an expensive campaign for the nomination in 1968, was considered a strong candidate, partly because he could prove that he was innocently banking and ranching in Uvalde when everybody was trading stock in Austin, his only state-government service having been as a legislator in the fifties. The favorite in the primary was Ben Barnes, the lieutenant governor, who had not been directly involved in the Sharpstown transactions, although, as David Broder of the Washington *Post* pointed out, all the talk about the number of investigations that had failed to link him with the scheme made him sound uncomfortably similar to Big Jule in "Guys and Dolls," who was renowned for having had thirty-three arrests, no convictions. (In the financial statement required of gubernatorial candidates, Barnes stated that he had two hundred and sixty-seven thousand dollars in assets—which, for a young man who had spent his entire career as a public servant at a salary even below that of the governor of Arkansas, displayed a degree of thrift that approached asceticism.) In winning the lieutenant governorship, Barnes, a protégé of Lyndon Johnson and John Connally, had carried every single one of the two hundred and fifty-four counties in Texas. His political rise was considered so inevitable that the two sides of a late-night political discussion about him in Austin could be divided by differing opinions on precisely which year he would become President of the United States.

The candidacy of Frances Farenthold seemed barely able to survive a description of who she was—a politically liberal woman who was called Sissy and had gone to Vassar and was married to a foreigner. (George Farenthold is a businessman who was born in Belgium and has been an American citizen since 1940. The George Farenthold, Jr., who was found murdered last week was his son by a previous marriage.) She was dismissed by all professional politicians as a token candidate who had absolutely no chance of making the runoff. In Austin, she was known for holding strong views and expressing them—which in the way professional politicians judge candidates for statewide office is like having a serious disease and developing complications. In 1969, a resolution commending Lyndon Johnson for his handling of the Presidency, including, presumably, his handling of the war in Vietnam, had divided the Texas House along strictly male-female lines—a hundred and forty-nine for, one opposed. Among all the legislators who believed that sooner or later there had to be a change in the Texas marijuana law, which now makes possession of marijuana a felony that can be punished by life imprisonment, Mrs. Farenthold was the one willing to become identified as an advocate of pot by introducing a bill that would have made first-offense possession a misdemeanor. She openly supported the farm workers' boycott of lettuce and refused to join the other candidates in reciting the dread effects of school busing. Early in the campaign, she called for the abolition of the Texas Rangers—an élite corps of the state police that many Texas Anglos think of as a symbol of proud Texas history and many Mexican-Americans in the southern part of the state think of as a symbol of Anglo oppression. (She later said she would settle for making South Texas off-limits to the Rangers.) Her supporters could think of hardly anything else she could do to offend the type of voters Texas candidates ordinarily cultivate, except, perhaps, to launch a vitriolic personal attack on John Wayne. But her most important identification was still as someone who had fought the corruption in Austin rather than tolerated it—the Den Mother of the Dirty Thirty. Dolph Briscoe, advertising that he was a man Texans could believe in, got forty-four per cent of the votes, almost winning the primary without a runoff. But Sissy Farenthold finished second, eliminating both the incumbent governor and the incumbent lieutenant governor from the race.

Whether the simple fact of being a woman gained or lost votes for Sissy Farenthold was a popular subject for discussion after the primary—the primary results having relieved the discussants of the burden of arguing about which year Ben Barnes would be President. There was some question whether a woman candidate was culturally unacceptable to a lot of Mexican-Americans or to those Texas Anglos whose idea of a public leader is the father of the Cartwrights on horseback. There was some question whether middle-class Anglo women found her a source of pride or envy. She had, after all, lived what might be the fantasy of any housewife who felt unfulfilled by the League of Women Voters: a lawyer from a family long prominent in Texas law, she had waited until her youngest child was in school before taking up full-time practice, and seven years later had found herself as a candidate for governor. There were those who believed that her unusually strong primary vote in normally conservative suburbs reflected the support of women, although other analysts traced it to simple snob appeal.

In the runoff campaign, being a woman gave Mrs. Farenthold certain advantages—all of them the kind of advantages that would strike a women's liberationist as reflections of a sexist society. Briscoe suffered from his refusal to meet her in debate, a refusal normally expected of a candidate who knows he has a large lead, mainly because it made him appear to be cowering before a woman. Mrs. Farenthold, who at one point trapped Briscoe in a Fort Worth hotel lobby to ask him about the debate face-to-face, often said that Briscoe was running away from her, and in speeches during the last week of the campaign she sometimes followed that accusation with a line that never failed to draw applause: "How unmanly!"

The singularity of a woman candidate was probably responsible for some of the television and newspaper coverage that made Mrs. Farenthold's name familiar to voters in an extraordinarily short time. At some point in the runoff campaign, Mrs. Farenthold became a star, and rallies would end with dozens of young people coming up to the platform to thrust forward posters on which she was expected to scrawl "Sissy." Outside Corpus Christi, she did not receive the endorsement of one major newspaper, but any news item about Dolph Briscoe seemed to be accompanied by two or three about Sissy Farenthold. The headlines usually referred to Briscoe formally by his last name and called Mrs. Farenthold Sissy, as if the reporter thought of him as some stiff banker suffering an interview and of her as a personal friend—which, as it happened, was usually the case. Just before the runoff voting, a labor lawyer who has become accustomed to finding word of his candidates somewhere back near the auction notices told an acquaintance that he first realized Mrs. Farenthold's appeal to the press after she made a routine trip to inspect the pollution in the Houston ship channel. (The ship channel may be best known to future historians not for the role it plays in Houston's economy but for a remark made in defense of its cleanliness. When environmentalists were being particularly critical a year or so ago about what some factories were dumping into the water, one official tried to put it all into perspective by telling a reporter that arsenic is a scare word.) "At breakfast the next morning, I picked up the paper and there was a three-column headline saying 'Sissy Astonished at Pollution in Ship Channel,'" the labor lawyer said. "Three columns! I said, 'Well, the Lord is with us this time.'" On the day the conservative Dallas *Morning News* endorsed Briscoe on its editorial page, its two interpretive pieces on the campaign were headlined "Briscoe Strategy Barring Full Coverage by Press" and "Sissy Shoulders Burden of Stardom with Aplomb."

Despite their reputation for being embattled, liberals in Texas are not just a tiny minority, as they would be in, say, Mississippi. When their traditional coalition of labor and the minorities and ideological liberals is operating, they can carry the state—which hasn't happened in the governor's race for many years but has accounted for the election of Ralph Yarborough to the Senate a few times. The two or three people who told Sissy Farenthold that she had a chance of making the runoff based their prediction not on her appeal as a reformer but on what they called a "structural opportunity"—a number of liberal votes that no other candidate was likely to get. She went into the runoff without the official endorsement of the state labor organization and without assurance of a large turnout of black and Mexican-American voters. But her advisers hoped she could make up the difference with the support of young voters and women and, most of all, people of all sorts of backgrounds who were disgusted with the state government and wanted reform.

It is routine for Texas candidates who can be labelled liberals to assure voters that old labels like "liberal" and "conservative" are meaningless. Mrs. Farenthold managed to sound more persuasive than most, partly because of her approach—she seemed to be considering each issue separately rather than fitting it into some ideological framework—and partly because of the issue that brought her to prominence. Although the Dirty Thirty had included the liberal faction in the House, it had also included some Democrats who were not liberals and even some Republicans. Mrs. Farenthold, campaigning as a reformer rather than a liberal, maintained that the issue of the campaign was public government versus private government rather than liberal versus conservative. Compared to what she was accused of believing about marijuana and busing and abortion, her concentration on the need to end favoritism and bring honest representation to Austin sometimes sounded like a respectable, middle-class appeal for good government. But if public government actually ever did replace private government in Austin—if, as Mrs. Farenthold suggested, the lobbyists were reduced to the role of petitioners rather than manipulators—the result would have been the "radical upheaval" Briscoe accused Mrs. Farenthold of favoring. The manipulators she was talking about represent the most powerful financial interests in the state. What the Democrats who have always defeated the liberals in statewide races have had in common is not a rigid political ideology—a number of them, including Ben Barnes, are noted for their flexibility—but a compassion for the plight of people who have to wake up every morning and face the problems of running an oil company or a bank or a utility.

Briscoe, in a cautious campaign restricted pretty much to television and newspaper advertisements, said that the reform issue had been settled in the first primary. As most voters perceive the need for reform—ending personal corruption rather than tampering with corporate control—he was right. The incumbent governor had been badly defeated, after all, and the Speaker of the House had eventually been convicted of conspiracy to commit bribery. The line that always drew the most applause at one of Mrs. Farenthold's speeches—that the governor's chair was not for sale this year—expressed a view that cost Briscoe no votes among voters who were interested in reform. As a matter of personal corruption, it made no difference that, as Mrs. Farenthold often said during the campaign, Briscoe had already begun to deal with the same lobbyists she had been fighting. In the traditional view of reform, Briscoe had the same qualification that is often mentioned about a Rockefeller who runs for governor in a place like Arkansas or West Virginia or New York—"He's too rich to steal."

—1972

MOLLY IVINS, R.I.P.

In her columns Molly could, of course, make you laugh out loud, but that gift for humor may have masked some of her other talents. Occasionally—for instance, in her column about a visit to the Vietnam War memorial that brought back memories of a young man whose name is etched on that wall—she could make you cry. She could see through phoniness at long distances. The week after she died, Paul Krugman of the *New York Times* searched through the columns she'd done from Austin at a time when most of the Washington press corps was swallowing the Bush administration's case for a war that would leave us triumphant in the Middle East. In January of 2003, she wrote, "I assume we can defeat Hussein without great cost to our side. (God forgive me if that is hubris.) The problem is what happens after we win. The country is 20 percent Kurd, 20 percent Sunni and 60 percent Shiite. Can you say, 'Horrible three-way civil war?'" Here's what she wrote that October: "I've got an even-money bet out that says more Americans will be killed in the peace than in the war and more Iraqis will be killed by Americans in the peace than in the war. Not the first time I've had a bet out that I hoped I'd lose."

Whatever talents she had in other areas, though, she was born to cover Texas politics. She had a spectacular command of the vernacular, and she took an infectious joy in the show. It was Molly who wrote that if a certain congressman's IQ dropped any further he'd have to be watered twice a day. It was Molly, in search of that telling detail, who reported that a Texas gubernatorial candidate was so afraid of getting AIDS while visiting San Francisco that when he was in the shower he wore shower caps on his feet. The picture of Molly that lingers in the mind is her finishing a discourse on some bizarre activities of a legislator from Big Spring or Uvalde, and then saying, after a great laugh, "Ain't he a caution!"

Those of us who adored her adored her not for her formidable talents but for the sort of person she was. Her interest in helping the powerless was as genuine as her contempt for the public officials who concentrated on helping the powerful. Her loyalty had no bounds and no statute of limitations; no matter which journalistic organization actually paid her salary, I believe she was always, in her heart, Molly Ivins of the *Texas Observer.* Reporters visiting Texas on a political story got from Molly not resentment about intrusion on her turf but a jolly welcome to pull up a chair and watch what she referred to as "the finest form of free entertainment ever invented."

She was fantastic company. When you caught sight of her at a political convention, you realized that you were going to have some fun regardless of how long the speeches went on. When the *Nation* magazine's cruise stopped in St. Thomas, the thought of spending the day in what is essentially a shopping mall with sun could be brightened by Molly organizing an expedition looking for what she called, as I remember, slutty shoes.

She responded to having cancer the way you would have expected her to. If there's anything a Texas liberal knows about, it's continuing to fight even when the odds are stacked against you. When she was given an award in New York not that long ago, she used her acceptance speech to tell the story of trying to find a prosthetic breast in Paris, hers having been lost in some misdirected luggage. As I remember Molly's description of her efforts to communicate, the French phrase she used for prosthetic breast was something like "that from which the baby sucks, except a false one of that from which the baby sucks," and the items offered by puzzled clerks included a baby bottle and a glass eye. In other words, she cussed cancer and she analyzed cancer and, being Molly, she even made fun of cancer. Weren't she a caution!

—2007

CREDITS

"Not Super-Outrageous," copyright © 1970 by Calvin Trillin. Originally appeared in the *New Yorker*.

"Three Texans in Six Lines" originally appeared in the *Nation*. © 1993, 1999, 2005 by Calvin Trillin.

"Making Adjustments," copyright © 1984 by Calvin Trillin. Originally appeared in the *New Yorker*.

"Presidential Ups and Downs: Washington Pundits Take Their Analytical Skills to the Ranch" (originally entitled "Life on the Ranch"), copyright © 2001 by Calvin Trillin. Originally appeared in the *New Yorker*.

"The Life and Times of Joe Bob Briggs, So Far," copyright © 1986 by Calvin Trillin. Originally appeared in the *New Yorker*.

"One Texan in Eight Lines" (originally entitled "Phil Gramm Says We're a Nation of Whiners"), copyright © 2008 by Calvin Trillin. Originally appeared in the *Nation*.

"Reformer," copyright © 1972 by Calvin Trillin. Originally appeared in the *New Yorker*.

"Molly Ivins, R.I.P.", by Calvin Trillin. Eulogy read at memorial service in 2007.